AI-Based Plant Disease Detection Using Deep Convolutional Neural Networks

Nancy Kova

Table of Contents

Chapter 3

Diagnosis Of Cucumber Diseases by Plant Leaf Using A Deeper CNN Architecture

Chapter 4

A Hybrid Deep Convolutional Neural Network (DCNN) for Coffee Leaf Illness Classification

Chapter 6
A Hybrid Method For Detecting Corn Leaf Diseases Using ResNet and Capsule Neural Networks

Chapter 7
Conclusion and Future Work

CHAPTER 1

INTRODUCTION

There are several vital advantages that plants offer to both the natural realm and human existence. For most living things, including humans, to survive, plants are essential for the production of oxygen through photosynthesis. Through retaining carbon within their tissues and soil, they mitigate climate change by absorbing carbon dioxide into the atmosphere and lowering greenhouse gas emissions. Plants provide a wide variety of fruits, vegetables, grains, nuts, and seeds that are vital for human nutrition when used as a primary food source. Compounds found in many plants are utilized in both conventional and alternative medicine to treat a various type of illnesses and ailments.

Apart from preserving soil fertility and halting soil erosion, plant roots also promote sustainable agriculture. They also encourage nutrient cycling and improve soil structure. Plants maintain ecological stability and biodiversity by producing habitats and supplying food for a various type of organisms. Through soaking pollutants, filtering fine particles, and generating clean oxygen, they enhance air quality and promote healthier surroundings. Plants affect both local and global weather by controlling humidity and temperature through transpiration.

Plants are the source of raw materials for a wide range of businesses, including paper, textiles, biofuels, wood, and cosmetics, all of which promote economic expansion and advancement. By providing areas for leisure, relaxation, and aesthetic delight, they enhance the beauty of both urban and natural settings and promote mental health. Worldwide, plants are deeply ingrained in customs, traditions, and rituals that shape the fabric of culture and personality.

Plants are vital to preserving ecological balance and sustaining life on Earth because they provide vital ecosystem services like pollination, water filtration, and climate regulation. In general, plants provide vital functions that support life, enhance wellbeing, and maintain ecosystems, making them critical to the wellness of the earth and human cultures.

1.1 Plant disease introduction

Plant illness identification using leaf images are a vital task in precision agriculture. Detecting plant diseases using advanced techniques involves leveraging various technological advancements in image processing, Convolution Neural Network (CNN). Machine learning, and artificial intelligence [1], [2].

Plant diseases are described as any anomalous state that modifies the appearance or functionality regarding a plant. This physiological mechanism affects most, if not all, of the functions of plants. Additionally, disease can reduce the harvest's production and quality products so we can say that disease is an evolving process of change.

Symptoms are the outward signs of a disease that affect plants. Any discernible changes in a plant's colour, form, or functionality that arise from a pathogen or disease-causing substance are called symptoms. Leaf spots or blights, tissue fading, stunted growth, and withering are a few examples of symptoms. These signs could be localized to certain parts of the plant or present throughout.

While certain symptoms may point to a specific illness, the same or similar symptoms might be caused by several different microorganisms. Furthermore, symptoms frequently change over time, and environmental factors might have an impact on how they present. The physical evidence of the pathogen, or indications of plant illness, can help identify diseases in plants such as corn, cucumber, coffee, and pumpkin.

Living organisms that attack plants and feed on them are the source of infectious plant diseases. A pathogen is the parasitic organism that is the cause of a disease. The word "host" describes the plant that the pathogen has invaded and is using as a food source. In this case, the host is the soybean or corn plant.

Pathogens have the ability to spread illness and cause infection. Plant pathogens include nematode juveniles or adults, bacterial cells, fungal spores, and viral particles. The most prevalent plant pathogens are fungi.

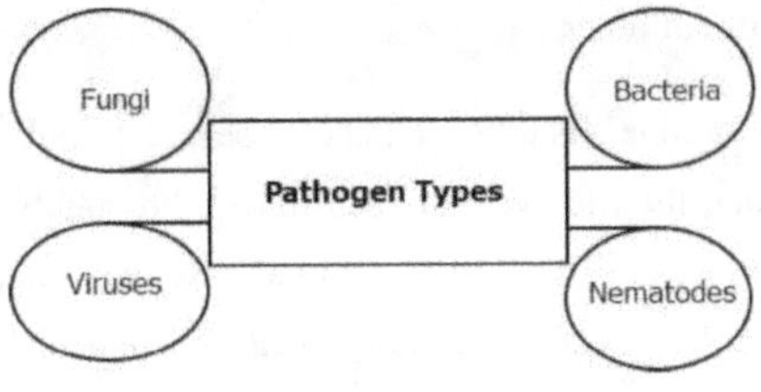

Figure 1.1 Pathogen Types

1.1.1. Plant disease triangle

All three components of the disease triangle have to be present at the same time for a plant disease to manifest: The plant, or host, must be vulnerable to the infection. Pathogen (e.g. the pathogen needs to exist and have the ability to infect the host. Environment: The conditions in which the pathogen grows and becomes infected must be favourable. A lack of any one of these components prevents the illness from progressing. By focusing on one or more triangle components, this idea aids in the comprehension and management of plant diseases. Figure 1.2 representing disease triangle.

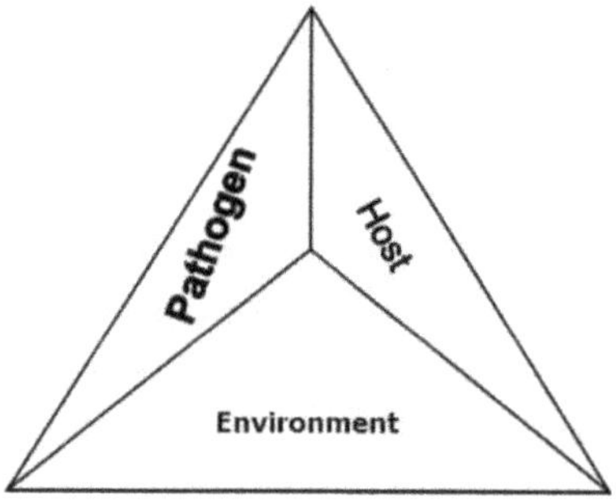

Figure 1.2 Plant disease triangle

1.1.2. Plant Disease Cycle

Conditions contribute to the disease cycle, resulting in the gradual progression of the illness. The creation of the inoculum, its dissemination to a host that is susceptible, its penetration into the host, infection, secondary cycles, and the pathogen's survival between hosts plants are the fundamental processes in the majority of disease cycles. Since management approaches frequently focus on particular phases of the disease's development, an understanding of the disease cycle is essential to effectively managing any illness. Reversing the cycle of disease can stop or lessen the onset of illness.

The aim of managing plant illness is to break the disease's cycle and prevent it from finishing completely. Understanding the life cycle of each illness thoroughly is essential for making effective management decisions. The term "inoculum" here refers to a pathogen's potentially infectious components, such as bacterial and fungal cells. The inoculum spreads by movement, and infection happens when the pathogen enters the host plant.

1.1.3. Role of environment of plant diseases

Plant diseases are greatly influenced by their surroundings in terms of their prevalence, growth, and dissemination. Farmers and other agricultural professionals can ensure healthier crops and more environmentally friendly farming methods by developing more effective disease prevention and control tactics by knowing and regulating environmental conditions.

1.2 Problem Statement

In forestry and cultivation, plant illness are a major source of production losses and financial losses. For instance, infections that affect cucumbers, like Powdery mildew and Downy mildew, have caused large monetary losses. Nowadays, agricultural land serves as a major economic contributor in addition to being a food origins. The economy of India is primarily reliant on agriculture and its products. The primary reason of agricultural yield loss is the existence of insects or other illnesses; hence, by providing a disease detection solution in agriculture, the risk of production losses may be reduced. Observations have shown that methods based on deep learning used for detecting diseases are becoming more and more significant in AI-based agricultural research [1], [2].

Deep learning provides effective methods for identifying plant diseases, improving agricultural operations' precision, effectiveness, and scalability. It is an invaluable tool for contemporary agriculture because of its capacity to automate and simplify disease monitoring and management.

However, the advantages of these methods are not fully realized in certain circumstances because of excessive expenditures and in other cases because of a lack of resilience. The present work uses hybrid approaches, deep learning and transfer learning models to effectively recognize and categorize plant sickness in spite of these challenges. In addition, early filtering techniques such as the Gabor filter approach collect more precise image data.

The suggested hyper heuristic-based method offers an automated, precise, and effective way to classify and identify plants leaf diseases, which is a substantial development in agricultural technology. The technology ensures healthier crops, more yields, and fewer financial losses by identifying illnesses in their early stages, which promotes more profitable and sustainable farming methods.

1.3 The problem's motivation

Plant identification provides a robust and accurate solution for identifying plant species. Various deep learning architectures allows for effective training of very deep models, capturing intricate details and patterns in plant images [3].By leveraging the global context Vision Transformers (ViTs)for automated plant disease classification provides a powerful and flexible solution for recognising plant illness [4].In this type of problem Image classification problems are a great fit for CNN, making them appropriate for detecting diseases in plant leaves [5].Agriculture could be completely changed by automatically detecting bacterial and fungal plant leaf problems using image processing and ML techniques. It makes early and precise diagnosis possible, which reduces crop losses and maximizes agricultural output. Regarding to overcome obstacles and take advantage of technology breakthroughs for sustainable agriculture and food security, this field has to continue researching and innovating [6].These approach can greatly improve the identification accuracy, classification and robustness of diagnosis of an illness, benefiting farmers and agricultural experts Hence, To guarantee greater crop yield and quality, automated and precise plant disease detection is crucial.

1.4 Types of Diseases in various plants

Biotic and abiotic diseases are the two main categories into which plant diseases can be divided.

1.4.1 Biotic Plant Diseases

Pathogens, which are living organisms that infect and consume nutrients in the host plant, are the cause of biotic illnesses. Typical biotic pathogens consist of:

- **Fungi:** A various type of plant Fungi are the cause of diseases. Powdery mildew, Downy mildew and Rust are a few examples.
- **Bacteria:** Bacterial blight, wilt, and spot are diseases caused by bacterial infections.
- **Viruses:** Diseases such mosaic viruses, which cause a mottling and deformation of leaves, are brought on by viral infections.
- **Nematodes:** These tiny worms can harm plant roots and general health by causing cyst infections and root knots.
- **Phytoplasmas:** Pathogenic microorganisms with specialized characteristics resembling bacteria that cause deadly yellowing and aster yellows.

1.4.2 Abiotic Plant Diseases

Environmental elements that are not living but have an adverse effect on plant health are the source of abiotic illnesses. Among these are:

- **Nutrient Deficiencies:** Reduced growth, chlorosis, and low yield can result from a deficiency in important nutrients like as potassium, phosphate, or nitrogen.
- **Water Stress:** Plants can suffer from both too little water and too much water, which can cause symptoms including wilting, root rot, and leaf burn.
- **Temperature Extremes:** A few temperature-related problems that might affect plants are frost damage, heat stress, and sunscald.
- **Imbalanced Soil pH:** Poor plant growth can arise from imbalanced soil pH, which can also impact nutrient availability and root health.
- **Physical Damage:** Pathogens and stress plants can enter through mechanical wounds caused by wind, hail, or human activity.

Both kinds of plant diseases have the Likelihood to have a major Influence on health, yield and general productivity of agricultural plants. Understanding the causes, symptoms, and suitable mitigation techniques for biotic and abiotic diseases is essential for effective disease management.

1.4.3 Plant Diseases caused by microorganism

Microorganism-caused plant diseases include a broad spectrum of pathogens include fungus, nematodes, viruses and bacteria. These diseases could cause major damage to crops, lower harvests, and compromise food security. Here are a few instances of plant illnesses brought on by various microorganisms:

1) **Fungal Diseases:** Fungal illnesses may have a substantial influence on the quality, productivity, and health of plants. Crop rotation, resistant types, adequate spacing for ventilation, fungicide spraying, and the removal and destruction of sick plant material are examples of effective management techniques. Anthracnose, powdery mildew, and downy mildew are a few common types of fungal disease found in plants.

2) **Bacterial Diseases:** Pathogenic bacteria that infect and feed on the host plant are the source of bacterial illnesses in plants, causing a various type of symptoms and harm. Among the frequent bacterial illnesses are: Bacterial Spot on Leaves and Fire Blight.

3) **Viral Diseases:** RNA or DNA genetic material covered in a protein shell makes up viruses, which are microscopic infectious agents. These agents can cause viral illnesses in plants. These viruses enter plant cells, use their reproductive machinery to proliferate, and then disperse throughout the plant to cause a various type of symptoms that can influence the health, growth, and gain of the plant as a whole. Among the frequent bacterial illnesses are: Mosaic Viruses, Wilt and Blight Viruses, Ring spot Viruses, and Necrosis and Lesion Viruses.

The causes, symptoms and management of most common diseases of plants are mentioned in Table 1.1.

Name of diseases	**Cause**	**Symptoms**	**Management**
Powdery Mildew	Fungi (such as Sphaerotheca and Erysiphe species)	Spots of white powder on stems, flowers, and foliage.	Apply fungicides, make sure there is adequate air circulation, use resistant types, and refrain from overhead watering.
Downy Mildew	Oomycetes (such as species of Plasmopara and Peronospora)	On the upper leaf surfaces, there are yellow or white patches; the underside has grayishmold.	Employ fungicides, enhance air circulation, choose resistant cultivars, and stay away from too much wetness.
Anthracnose	Fungi, such as species of Colletotrichum	Lesions on fruits, stems, and foliage that are dark and sunken.	Rotate your crops, use fungicides, and choose resistant cultivars.
Bacterial Spot on Leaves	Members of the Xanthomonas genus of bacteria (often has an impact on Solanaceae plants, such as tomatoes and peppers).	There is a noticeable defoliation and little, areas on the leaves that are wet that are encircled by a yellow halo here spots get larger and eventually turn brown or black.	Crop rotation using non-host plantsTake out and kill any sick plants.To enhance air circulation, make sure plants are spaced appropriately apart.Steer clear of overhead irrigation.

Fire Blight	Plants of the Rosacea family are primarily affected by the bacteria Erwiniaamylovora.	Dark green sores drenched in water on flowers, Necrotic patches on branches and brown or black, wilting, infected tissues.	Pruning, disinfection, avoiding high nitrogen fertilization, copper sprays, antibiotics, and biological control.
Mosaic Virus	Viruses (such as the Cucumber and Tobacco mosaic viruses)	Leaves with patches of light and dark green, mottled or striped, and stunted development.	Utilize virus-free seeds, eradicate afflicted plants, manage insect vectors, and maintain proper hygiene.
Wilt and Blight Viruses	Fungi, such as Alternaria and Phytophthora species also bacteria such as Erwinia species.	Leaf tissue quickly and extensively browns and dies.	Employ fungicides or bactericides, use resistant cultivars, and make sure your crops are rotated well.
Ring spot Viruses	Ring spot viruses can spread through Aphids and Nematodes,	Symmetrical or asymmetrical leaf discolouration patterns, Yellowing of the surrounding areas, death of plant tissues, and slowed growth are possible.	Removing and eliminating the contaminated plant, Rotate sensitive crops and use the right fertilizer, irrigation, and pest control techniques.
Necrosis and Lesion Viruses	Exacerbated by fluctuations in humidity, temperature, and nutrient deficiencies.	Discreet or irregular patches of dead tissue on leaves, The leaf tissue around the lesions may turn yellow or brown, and the leaves themselves may sag.	Combination of vector control, sanitation, and the adoption of resistant cultivars.

Table 1.1 Common disease of plants their symptoms and cure

1.4.4 Sample of Plant Disease caused by microorganism

1) **Cucumber Leaf diseases:** Numerous diseases that can seriously affect production and quality can affect cucumber plants. These include angular leaf spot, mimic

viruses, powdery mildew, and downy mildew among other common cucumber illnesses.

2) **Coffee Leaf diseases:** Numerous illnesses that might seriously hinder a coffee plant's growth and productivity can affect it. Diseases known as Coffee Leaf Rust, Brown Eye Spot, Coffee Diseases of the Coffee Berry (CBD) and Coffee Wilt (CWD) are a few prevalent diseases that afflict coffee plants.
3) **Pumpkin Leaf diseases:** Pumpkin plants are prone to several illnesses that may affect their productivity and overall health. The following are some prevalent illnesses that impact pumpkin plants: bacterial wilt, powdery mildew, downy mildew and anthracnose.
4) **Corn Leaf diseases:** Numerous diseases affect corn, a staple crop that is cultivated worldwide, and can adverse effect on both production and quality. Following are some typical diseases that afflict corn plants: corn smut, typical rust and Corn leaf bligh in the north and south as well as grey leaf spot.

1.5 Introduction of Hyper-Heuristic Method for Plant Illness Identification and Classification

Early and precise identification of plant illness is necessary. It diseases pose major threats to world agriculture because they have an effect on agricultural productivity, quality, and food security effectively manage and avoid significant agricultural losses. Plant disease identification through visual inspection by specialists requires a lot of work on time-consuming, and frequently prone to errors in the process. Plant disease identification and classification have undergone a revolutionary change in recent years thanks to the integration of sophisticated computer vision and ML techniques. To get the best results, these methods frequently need to be carefully adjusted and parameters and algorithms chosen.

A hyper-heuristic approach presents a viable way to tackle these issues. High-level search techniques called hyper-heuristics are designed to automate the process of choosing, combining, and creating heuristics in order to tackle challenging optimization issues. As opposed to conventional heuristics, which concentrate on particular problem cases, hyper-heuristics function more broadly, improving flexibility and adaptability.

A strong and adaptable structure for classifying and identifying of plant diseases is provided by the hyper-heuristic method. Hyper-heuristics improve disease detection systems' accuracy, efficiency, and resilience by automating the optimization of models and parameters. This strategy has a great deal of promise to advance environmental sustainability, guarantee food security, and enhance agricultural practices. The field of modern agriculture is about to undergo a transformation as hyper-heuristic methodology advances and become more and more integrated into plant disease detection systems.

1.5.1 Role of hyper heuristic approach in plant illness identification and classifications

Plant illness identification and categorization can benefit significantly from the use of hyper-heuristic approaches, which offer an adaptable and flexible framework for maximizing the effectiveness of ML models. Here are some crucial facets of its function:

1) **Meta-Optimization:** Hyper-heuristics concentrate on the creation and selection of heuristics, functioning at a higher level than conventional heuristics. This implies that a hyper-heuristic can optimize the selection of parameters and algorithms to raise the accuracy and efficiency of classifying diseases models in plant disease identification.
2) **Adaptability:** The image quality, disease symptoms, and environmental aspects of datasets related to plant diseases can differ significantly. By dynamically choosing the best heuristic or set of heuristics for a particular dataset, hyper-heuristics can adjust to these fluctuations.
3) **Automation:** By automating the model selection and parameter tuning processes, hyper-heuristics can lessen the requirement for human interaction and specialized knowledge. This is especially helpful in agricultural contexts where there may not be as much experience with machine learning and plant pathology. Efficiency: Hyper-heuristics can cut down on the time and computational resources needed to create plant disease detection models by streamlining the search for the optimum heuristics. As a result, models may be implemented into practical agricultural applications more quickly.
4) **Robustness:** By avoiding over fitting and guaranteeing that the models perform well when applied to fresh, unforeseen data, hyper-heuristics can strengthen the robustness of plant disease detection models. In order to build dependable systems that can manage the variety of plant illnesses and environmental circumstances, this is essential.

5) **Scalability:** Hyper-heuristics are appropriate for application in substantial agricultural operations because they can scale to huge and complex datasets. They offer a complete solution for plant health monitoring since they can manage a various type of plant species and disease types.

1.5.2 Realistic Application

1) **Feature Selection:** To improve the accuracy of disease classification models, hyper-heuristics can be utilized to derive the most pertinent features from photos of plants. This entails assessing several feature combinations and choosing the ones that have the greatest impact on precise categorization.
2) **Model Selection:** To determine which machine learning model is optimal for a given plant disease detection job, a variety of models (like ANN, CNN, SVM and Decision Trees) can be assessed and optimized using hyper-heuristics.
3) **Parameter Tuning:** To make sure that machine learning models run at peak efficiency, hyper-heuristics can automate the hyper parameter tuning process.
4) **Ensemble approaches:** To increase overall accuracy and resilience in plant disease detection, hyper-heuristics can optimize ensemble approaches by choosing and merging various models.
5) **Real-Time Monitoring:** Hyper-heuristics in precision agriculture can be included into real-time monitoring systems to continually optimize and adjust disease detection models in response to fresh field data.

1.5.3 Examples of Identification and Categorization of Plant Illness

To improve the models for identifying diseases of corn, cucumber, coffee, and pumpkin, we have used a hyper-heuristic method in this thesis study. As an example:

1) **Transfer Learning for Cucumber Diseases:** By optimizing the choice of trained models and adjusting parameters, a hyper-heuristic can enhance the transfer learning procedure.
2) **Hybrid Model for Coffee Diseases:** By maximizing the integration of Inception-V and Dense-Net architectures, a hyper-heuristic may ascertain how best to integrate them for improved classification accuracy.

3) **Feature Enhancement for Pumpkin Diseases:** The constitutive artificial neural network's architecture and the Gabor filter's parameters can be optimized using a hyper-heuristic.
4) **Hybrid Approach for corn Diseases:** By combining Res-Net and capsule neural networks in an optimal way, a hyper-heuristic may guarantee that the hybrid model functions well against a variety of maize leaf diseases.

Utilizing hyper-heuristics can help us enhance the efficacy, precision, and versatility of models for recognizing and categorizing plant illnesses increasing their usefulness in practical agricultural settings.

1.6 Recognition and Categorization of Plant Illness methods

Methods for recognising and classifying plant illness include a various approaches from sophisticated algorithms for DL and ML methods to conventional image processing. There are some important approaches identifying and classify plant diseases representing in Figure 1.3 and detailed description explained in following section.

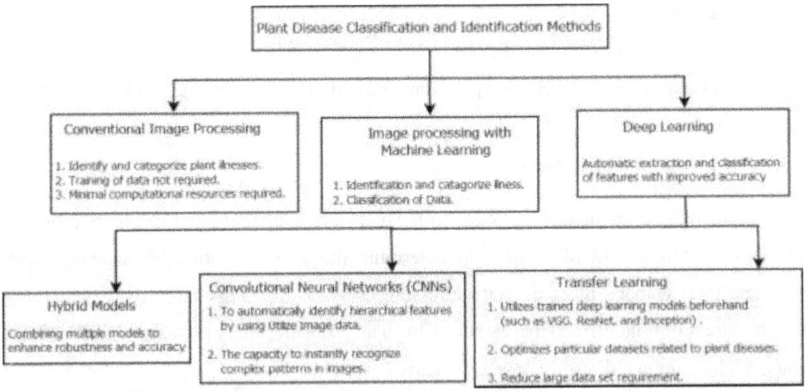

Figure 1.3 Different approaches used for plant Identifying and categorizing diseases

1.6.1 Detecting Plant Diseases using Image Processing

The two primary analyses in conventional image processing are texture analysis and colour analysis. Colour histograms and colour indices can be used as the basis for colour analysis.

With the use of texture analysis and colour histogram determine sickness symptoms of photos based on comparison with healthy images, plant stress can be identified using the Normalized Difference Vegetation Index (NDVI).Local binary patterns, or LBP, are the local contrast surrounding each pixel in this instance for texture analysis.

Plant disease categorization and detection heavily rely on image processing. Pre-processing, analysing, and interpreting picture data are the first steps in effectively identifying plant disease symptoms. An outline of the primary techniques for image processing applied in this field is provided below:

1) **Sources of Image Acquisition**
- Digital cameras: Sharp, precise images from high-resolution cameras.
- Tablets and smartphones: Practical for fieldwork.
- Drones: For extensive field observation.

2) **Preparing and Enhancing Images**
- Increases the appearance of illness signs.
- Noise reduction through the application of median filter, bilateral filter, and Gaussian blur techniques.
- Improves delicate details and edges.
- Pixel value scaling and colour space transformation, such as converting RGB to HSV and grayscale.

3) **The Extraction of Features**

Colour characteristics include colour distribution and statistical analysis of colour distribution. Features of Texture: GLCM is used to determine the spatial relationship between pixel intensities. Uses Gabor Filters to analyse texture at particular frequencies and orientations. Local texture information can be captured by using Local Binary Patterns (LBP). Shape features include things like border and geometric detection.

4) **Disease Detection**

The affected area is estimated to determine the disease severity once the segmentation approach has successfully detected the diseased regions in the leaf or fruit. The image processing steps for identification of plant disease shown in figure 1.4.

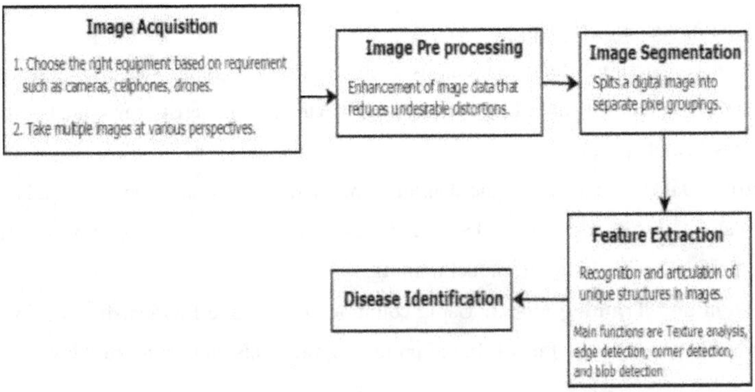

Figure 1.4 Required steps of Image processing for illness detection

1.6.2 Image Processing using Machine Learning

The combination of ML and image processing improves the accuracy of plant illness detection and classification. The convergence of ML and image processing creates novel opportunities across multiple domains. We can improve decision-making processes, automate image analysis jobs and extract information that is helpful from visual data by utilizing ML techniques. As long as scientists keep coming up with new and improved machine learning methods for image processing, we may anticipate more breakthroughs that will change the way we work with and interpret visual data.

A well-defined set of procedures representing in Figure 1.5, ranging from data collection and pre-processing to model training, assessment, and deployment, are involved in ML for image identification and classification. To guarantee the precision, effectiveness, and resilience of the finished classification system, each stage is essential. One can create efficient and dependable models for various images classification tasks, such as identifying plant diseases by carefully adhering to these stages. Description of these steps are as follows:

1) Acquiring Data: Identify the images that need to be collected for the work at hand. Gather the images into a structured dataset and, if necessary, divide it into several classes (such as healthy versus diseased or different forms of disease).

2) Data Preparation: Variety of improvement of training dataset and minimize over fitting, certain operations must be performed, including image resizing, pixel normalization, using filters to remove noise from images, and data augmentation (rotation, flipping, zooming, and cropping).

3) Feature Extraction: Require methods such as edge detection, shape analysis, and texture analysis (such as Gabor filters) to manually extract characteristics that are pertinent to the classification problem.

4) Splitting Data: A segment of the data must be training Set's allocation (typically 70–80%), Validation Set (usually 10-15%) and Test Set (10–15%) to determine the final model's performance during ML model training.

5) Selection and Training model: Using common choices like Random forests, SVMs, and CNNs suitable models for ML based on the requirements and nature of the work can select.

6) Model Deployment: Include the model in a program or platform that lets people submit new images and get the results of their classification.

7) Prediction and Classification: In final step performance indicators evaluate the model and predict the image.

8) Model Assessment: Evaluates the model with reference to variables such as recall, accuracy, precision, F1-score, and confusion matrix.

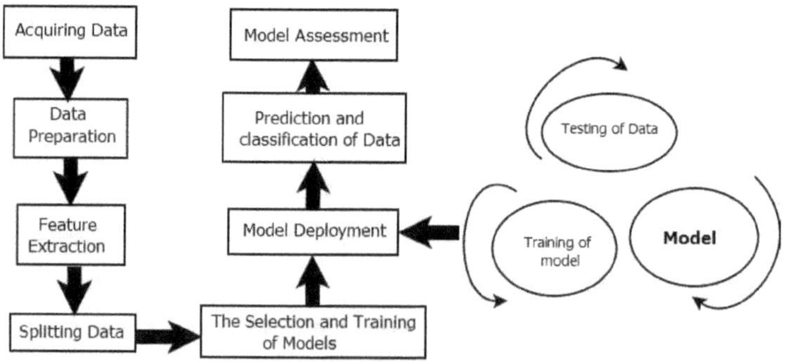

Figure 1.5 Steps in Image Processing with Machine Learning

1.6.3 Detection and Categorization of Plant Illness using Deep Learning

Deep learning has revolutionized the identification and Categorization of plant illness through offering strong tools for reliable classification and automatic feature extraction. Neural networks with convolutional layers (CNNs) and additional deep learning architectures have showed the capacity to precisely recognize and categorize plant illnesses from photos. There are three Deep learning algorithms for recognition and categorization of plant.

The methods listed below fall under deep learning.

I. Transfer Learning
II. Convolution neural Network(CNN)
III. Hybrid Models

I. Transfer Learning

Plant disease identification and classification can be done effectively and efficiently with the help of transfer learning. Smaller training datasets and less processing power are required to create reliable and accurate models by utilizing pre-trained models and optimizing them for certain purposes. This strategy can greatly improve farming methods, guaranteeing healthier harvests and increased food security.

The Transfer Learning Workflow for the recognition and categorization of plant illnesses as follows:

1) Gathering and pre-processing data

First of all acquire healthy and diseases images of different plant is required than Compute pixel values effectively and explore information.

2) Selection and Training of Models

Select a pre-trained model rather than include new completely interconnected layers that are tailored to the goal of classifying plant diseases after removing the top layer after that acquire and refine the model.

3) Assessment and Implementation of Models

At last step utilization of the test dataset's accuracy and confusion matrix are required than if need develop a mobile app that farmers may use in the field than export the model.

The workflow diagram of plant illness transfer learning identification and categorisation representing in Figure 1.6.

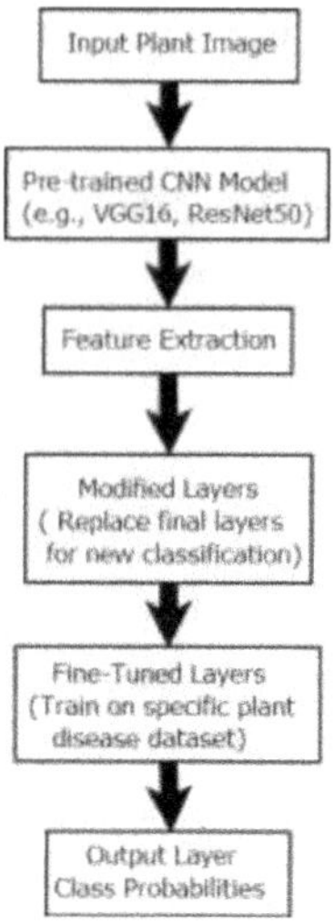

Figure 1.6 Work flow of Transfer Learning for the purpose of recognize and classify plant diseases

II. Plant Illness Identification and Categorization by using Convolutional Neural Networks

Plant illness recognition and categorization are done by Convolution Neural Networks (CNNs). CNNs can automatically identify hierarchical features in plant images and extract them. Below is a discussion of CNN's working methodology for classifying and detecting plant diseases.

Step 1: Gather a sizable collection of excellent plant photos, encompassing both healthy and diseased specimens.

Step 2: Normalize the pixel value after resizing the image data collection and making sure every image is the same size.

Step 3: Data Augmentation: In order to strengthen the model applies some changes like turning around, flipping cropping and brightness adjustments applied to enhance the variety of the dataset.

Step 4: In this stage, the CNN architecture is created and adjusted to the task's complexity. Three categories of common layers of convolutional, completely connected layers and pooling layers used in this work.

Step 5: There are three types of datasets: test, sets for both validation and training. After that, the CNN model is adjusted for hyper parameters by training on the practice field and validating on the set of validation.

Step 6: The model's performance is assessed by metrics efficacy on the test dataset that including precision, recall, F1 score and accuracy.

Step 7: This step involves optimizing the model through the use of regularization and pace of learning scheduling approaches, as well as hyper parameter adjustments.

The working flow diagram of for Using deep learning to recognize and categorization of plant illness is represent in Figure 1.7

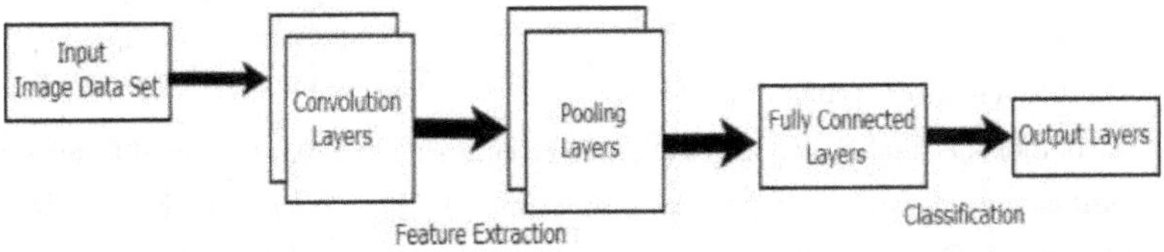

Figure 1.7 CNN Architecture for Recognizing and Categorising Plant Illnesses

The Advantages of Plant Illness Recognition and Classification using CNNs:

i. **Automated Feature Extraction:** With CNNs automatically extracting features from images, the necessity of manual feature extraction is eliminated.

ii. **High Accuracy:** CNNs can classify images with a high level of precision if they have access to enough data and have received the right training.

iii. **Scalability:** CNNs can be made to handle complicated issues with classification and large datasets.

Difficulties and Consideration:

i. **Quantity and Quality of Data:** CNNs require a great deal of well-labelled and superior quality data.

ii. **Computer Resources:** A substantial amount of computer resources, such as potent GPUs, are needed for CNN training, particularly when working with big datasets.

iii. **Over fitting:** If training data is not adequately regularized, CNNs may over fit the data. This can be lessened with the aid of strategies like dropout, data augmentation, and early ending.

III. Identification and Categorization of Plant Illnesses using Hybrid Models

Combining distinct ML and DL methods to capitalize on their advantages and enhance system performance is known as hybrid model plant disease detection and classification. Comparing hybrid models to individual models, hybrid models can offer superior generalization, resilience, and accuracy.

Important Elements of Hybrid Models:

i. Convolutional Neural Networks (CNNs) can be enhanced in the extraction of features and classification by combining them with other models, like Random Forests, SVM and Efficient Net.

ii. Feature fusion is the procedure for merging features from a number of models or techniques to produce a feature representation that is more thorough.

iii. Applying ensemble methods to combine the predictions of several models for increased accuracy, such as bagging, boosting, or stacking.

Sample Hybrid Models for Plant Disease Recognition and Categorization

i. Combination of CNN and SVM

SVMs should be used for classification and CNNs in order to extract features. While SVMs are capable of producing strong classification boundaries, CNNs excel in removing hierarchical features from images. Figure 1.8 representing overall working Hybrid model of SVM and CNN for classifying and recognising plant diseases.

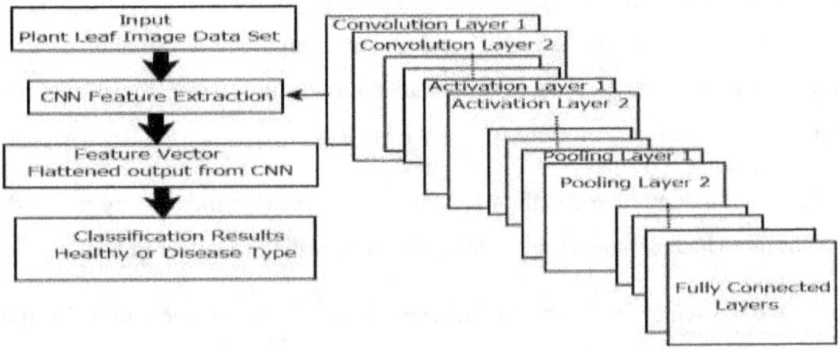

Figure 1.8 Workflow diagram of Hybrid Model of SVM and CNN for Plant Disease Recognition and Categorization

ii. Joint effect of Random Forest and CNN

In order to extract features, use CNNs, and for categorization, use Random Forests. High-dimensional feature spaces can be handled by Random Forests, which also offer resilience against over fitting. Detailed steps of discuss below represent in Figure 1.9.

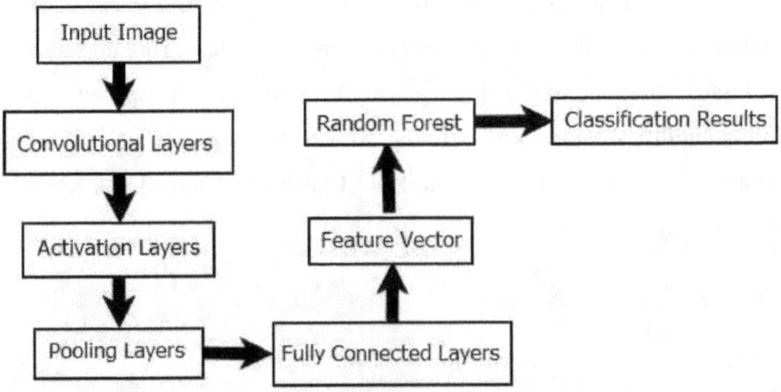

Figure 1.9 Workflow diagram of Hybrid Model of Random Forest and CNN for Plant Disease Recognition and Categorization

Step 1: The procedure starts in the input layer, where the system is fed images of both healthy and sick plant leaves.

Step 2: Many convolution layers use various filters applied to the image dataset for the purpose of derive feature maps from them. Non-linearity is introduced by the use of activation functions, such as ReLU. Feature maps are reduced via pooling layers (such as max pooling) to reduce dimensionality and preserve important information. A vector with a fixed length of features is created by flattening and processing the results of the last pooling layer through one or more fully linked layers.

Step 3: The Random Forest is then fed the feature vector generated by the CNN's fully linked layers, which captures the salient features regarding the input images.

Step 4: A vote with a majority among every decision tree in the forest determines the ultimate classification. A different collection of data points and features is utilized for training each of the decision trees that make up the Random Forest.

Step 5: The classification results are generated by the Random Forest, which also specifies the precise disease if the plant is unhealthy. These findings show either the plant is ill or well.

iii. Mixed Deep Learning Frameworks

Combine multiple deep learning architectures, such Inception with DenseNet or ResNet with Capsule Networks, to benefit from their complementary features.This approach combines a secondary classification network, like a Capsule Network (CapsNet), for improved classification capabilities with Convolutional Neural Networks (CNNs) for extraction of features. Figure 1.10 representing hybrid model of Capsule Net and other CNN model.

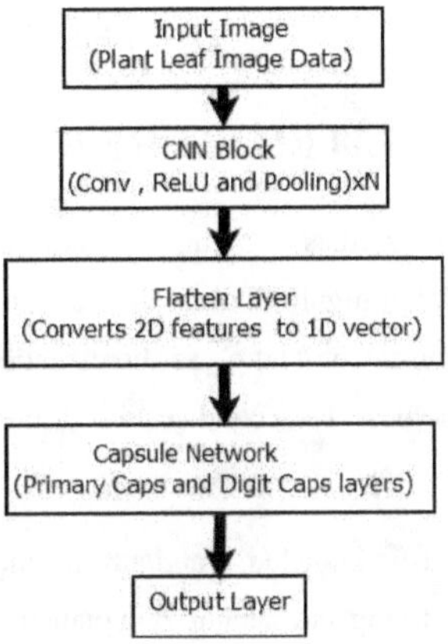

Figure 1.10 Hybrid model of Capsule Networks and other CNN's model for Plant Disease Recognition and Categorization

1.7 Thesis Outlines

This thesis comprises the following chapters:

Chapter 2: This chapter offers an extensive literature review, identifies research gaps, and outlines the research objectives.

Chapter 3: This chapter details the dataset, methods, and result analysis of the suggested deep CNN architecture-based model for identifying cucumber plant leaf illnesses.

Chapter 4: This chapter discusses the dataset, methods, and result analysis of the suggested hybrid deep CNN architecture for coffee disease classification.

Chapter 5: This chapter describes the dataset, methods, and result examination of the suggested hybrid approach for detecting corn leaf diseases using ResNet and capsule neural networks.

Chapter 6: This chapter covers the dataset, methods, and result examination of the suggested technique for identifying plant leaf illness in pumpkin plants using a constitutive artificial neural network with Gabor filters.

Chapter 7: This chapter presents the conclusion of the entire thesis work.

CHAPTER 2

LITERATURE REVIEW

This chapter includes useful studies on identifying and categorizing plant diseases using hyper heuristic approach in order to highlight areas that have not yet been thoroughly explored but may benefit from more research. There are three sections in this chapter: the first section reviews current methodologies; the second section discusses gap identification; and the third section discusses research aims.

The advancement of scientific knowledge and advancements in technology is reflected in the development method identifying and categorizing plant diseases. From prehistoric observations to advanced AI-driven models, the trip illustrates the ongoing efforts to safeguard crops and guarantee food security. The control of plant diseases in the future will depend on how cutting-edge technologies and multidisciplinary approaches are used to handle new problems in agriculture. These computer-based solutions have been included in the literature review from several peer-reviewed academic conferences and journals.

2.1 Review of Current Approaches

The advent of computer-based methods throughout the 1990s signified a turning point in the history categorization of plant illnesses and detection. We have studied several computer based technique to recognize and categorize plant illnesses and included these study in the form of peer reviewed journal, conferences and book series in this section.

2.1.1 Study of Digital Image Processing involved for Recognition of Plant Illness

The area of plant disease identification has greatly advanced thanks to digital image processing, which offers methods and tools for automating the diagnosis process. Researchers can precisely identify and categorize plant diseases through the collection and analysis of images, which enables prompt and efficient treatment strategies. The foundation of this technology is the integration of pre-processing, feature collection, segmentation and Categorization of images opening the door for more complex and scalable precision agriculture solutions.In this section, I discuss various methods of image processing for the identification of plant diseases, based on an analysis of multiple research articles.

In Mahlein, A. K. (2016), Authors discuss about Plant phenotyping and precision agriculture can both be improved with the help of imaging sensors. Although these domains utilize comparable technologies, they have unique needs that are customized for their respective uses. Accurate, scalable, real-time, and reasonably priced solutions that fit field circumstances are necessary for precision agriculture. Plant phenotyping, on the other hand, is more concerned with well-regulated conditions, high throughput, in-depth trait analysis, and repeatable experiments. For image sensor solutions to be developed effectively and satisfy the requirements of both areas, it is imperative to comprehend these similarities and specific demands [7].

In Khadabadi, et al.(2015),Authors introduce timely and accurate diagnosis of infections is necessary for a successful supervision of vegetable crops. For this reason, image processing techniques provide a solid solution by enabling automatic and effective illness identification. Using automation and accuracy, image processing techniques provide a potent tool for vegetable disease detection. Disease management can be made more effective and efficient by utilizing techniques like feature extraction, categorization, and preprocessing. The precision and adaptability of vegetable illness detection systems could be further improved by continuing to advance and integration of cutting-edge image processing techniques [8].

In Malathy et al. (2021), Authors discuss Techniques for image processing that automate and improve fruit disease detection accuracy by utilizing cutting-edge techniques in feature extraction, preprocessing, and classification, this work advances the creation of precise and automated systems for managing fruit diseases. A significant development in the area, the incorporation of such methods into farming procedures has an opportunity to enhance crop health and productivity [9].

In Manavalan (2021), Author present review paper that examines a number of computer methods for identifying illnesses in cucumber leaves. With a special emphasis on cucumber crops, the paper offers a thorough overview of the numerous methods and strategies utilized in the context of plant disease detection. This work provides useful information about the state of computational methods for illness detection in cucumber leaves at the moment. Early identification of cucumber infections is necessary to enhance yield. This causes the dosage control of pesticides to be inaccurate. To increase cucumber production and quality, disease detection and diagnosis must be automated. These algorithms diagnose infections early on by extracting information from images of cucumber plants. A summary of image processing and ML methods utilized for identifying illness in cucumber leaves. The future potential of computer algorithms for assessing images of cucumber leaves is also covered in this research. Through an overview of current methods and an identification of obstacles, the review provides a basis for further investigation and advancement in the domain [10].

Gabor filters are utilize in study of Nashrullah et al. (2021) for texture-based extraction of features to identifying tomato leaf illness. The usefulness of employing Gabor filters to the analysis of textural data suggestive of different leaf diseases is investigated in this research. Regarding the identification of plant illness, this work emphasizes the benefits of utilizing filtering with Gabor for texture-based feature extraction. The technique offers a thorough study that can raise the accuracy in disease diagnosis in tomato leaves by concentrating on textural patterns. This method helps to create instruments for plant health management that are more potent [11].

In Phadikar and Sil's (2008) work, illnesses in rice crops are identified by applying pattern recognition algorithms. The study focuses on using a variety of computer techniques to assess and categorize rice illnesses using pattern recognition. The work by Phadikar and Sil shows how pattern recognition methods can be utilized for identifying illnesses in rice crops. Through the utilization of computational techniques and visual patterns, the research provides insightful perspectives for enhancement of accuracy and efficiency of illness identification. By using these methods, rice crops are managed more effectively, and agricultural output is increased [12].

Various image processing approaches are utilize in Pooja et al. (2017) study to identify illnesses in plant leaves. For the purpose of improving plant health management researchers explores the use of these strategies to enhance the recognition and classification of leaf illness. This study demonstrates how well techniques for image processing work for diagnosing illnesses of the leaves of plants. The research offers important insights into enhancing the accuracy and efficacy of illness diagnosis. This is necessary for effective plant health management by concentrating on cutting-edge image analysis techniques [13].

In Prasad et al.(2012),Explores the application by the Gabor Wavelet Transform as a unique pattern recognition technique for crop disease identification. The three primary parts of the suggested plant biometric system are: (1) feature extraction by GWT, (2) feature matching with

SVM, a powerful machine learning technique, and (3) spot detection through histogram-based segmentation. According to experimental findings on a variety of disease datasets, GWT is a reliable and highly successful method for recognizing plant illness, with an accuracy of roughly 89% depending on the circumstances. In addition to being a useful tool for biology and botany research, the established system helps Indian farmers learn about diseases of crops and how to cure them using both chemical and natural methods, which increases agricultural yields [14].

Techniques for image processing are utilize in research of Prakash et al. (2017) to identify diseases of the leaves of plants. Utilizing an image assessment and categorization methods for classifying and identifying leaf diseases is the study's goal.

There are four parts to explore work:

1) Preprocessing of the image
2) Leaf segmentation to locate unhealthy areas utilizing K-means clustering
3) Feature extraction
4) Disease categorization.

A classification method employs SVM and leverages GLCM analysis to extract texture information [15].

Veerendra et al. (2022) evaluate techniques for leaf and stem identification in plants. Three modules comprise their approach: detection, categorization, and severity quantification. The main technological approaches applied in the algorithms are the basis for additional divisions within each module. Leaf diseases are diagnosed using these image processing techniques. They aid in the removal of diseased sections on citrus leaves and the appropriate classification of those leaves. Plant disease detection is improved by additional research and application to digital image processing methods. Agricultural management and greenhouses benefit from this strategy. Fruits, leaves, and stems are only a few of the elements of the plant that can be impacted by diverse bacteria and microbes [16].

In Kaur.P. et al. (2022), Suggested a technique of object identification model and the extraction of features architecture for tomato leaf illness detection based on profound CNN. To recognise tomato leaf illnesses, a combined neural network and the modified Mask R-CNN are utilized. Empirical findings, derived from publicly available data, suggested techniques are successfully and precisely identify several tomato illnesses and distinguish the morphology of the afflicted areas [17].

In Dai.G. et al. (2024) discuss that for support for several optimal deployment strategies and ability to balance recognition speed and accuracy YOLOv5 series of majority of research frequently starts with neural network models. YOLOv5, which first gained popularity in target detection-related computer vision tasks has mostly used in categorization, semantic, and segmentation applications [18].

In Singh, V. et al. (2020) Plant illnesses cause serious production losses and monetary losses for the global agriculture sector. Sustainable agriculture depends on the monitoring of plant and tree health and the early identification of illnesses. As far as we are aware, no commercially available sensor exists It can be utilized to evaluate a tree's health in real time. The most popular method for tracking stress in trees at the moment is scouting, which is a costly, labour-intensive and time-consuming procedure. Agriculture production is being actively increased by numerous individuals and groups. Numerous techniques have been attempted in the past to halt the disease's progress in plants [19].

In Karthik, K.,et al.(2021),Authors proposed image processing based on deep learning methods to identify plant leaf illness of two types of plant tomato and potato dataset and also introduce the common knowledge base concept for prediction of plant leaf illness [20].

2.1.2 Study on Image Processing utilizing Machine Learning to Recognize and Categorization of Plant Diseases

In Akben (2019), an important development in medical diagnostics is the application of data mining as well as expert systems to identify ranges of values for blood, hormones, and weight indicators linked to breast cancer [21].

In Tang, L. et al. (1999) describe how a two-layer Fourier extraction of features as well as neural network-based pattern recognition system was developed to categorize weed into grass and broadleaf classes in order to applying selective herbicides in actual time. This system replicated human visual system operations. The collaborative spatial-frequency properties of the images of weed textures were obtained through the application of Gabor wavelets. The functioning of visual cortex cells was replicated by using Gabor wavelets feature extractor [22].

A study of the effectiveness of deep neural networks (DNNs) for server-based computing in the classification various illnesses affecting tomato leaves is shown in Cholachgudda et al. (2021). The feasibility of using multiple models for deep learning to reliably diagnose distinct tomato leaf diseases is assessed in this work. The computing requirements associated with training and setting up these models is handled by server-based computing infrastructures. The performance measures of several neural network topologies and their applicability for real-world agricultural applications are covered in the article. The outcomes show that DNNs can classify illness with more accuracy when combined with server-based computing, providing a reliable solution for tomato crop monitoring and management in actual time [23].

To enhance the forecasting of purchase likelihood, Chu.S et al. (2021) present an adaptive convex clustering technique using generalized linear models (GLMs). In order to account for different kinds of response variables and cluster observations with comparable patterns, the method integrates the versatility of convex clustering along with the flexibility of GLMs. The method offers improved performance over conventional clustering algorithms and is especially helpful for forecasting consumer behavior and likelihood of purchase. This work contains theoretical analysis and uses computer simulations and real-life applications in likelihood of purchase prediction to demonstrate the efficacy of the proposed approach. According to the findings, the adaptable convex clustering method produces clusters that are more precise and understandable, which improves prediction accuracy in real-world situations [24].

The proposed method by Dhanaseelan & Sutha,(2021) uses frequent item sets mining techniques to uncover patterns linked to breast cancer, while fuzzy logic is used to address ambiguity and imprecision in medical data. The method seeks to enhance the precision of breast cancer recognition and categorization by fusing fuzzy reasoning with data mining technologies. The study assesses the efficacy of this approach using a variety of datasets, showing that it can diagnose breast cancer more precisely than more conventional approaches. According to the findings, fuzzy frequently used item sets mining offers a strong framework for deciphering intricate medical data and enhancing diagnostic precision [25].

The image processing method presented by Dubey & Jalal (2012) includes a number of crucial steps: First, picture segmentation is accomplished using the clustering algorithm K-Means technique. From the split image, advanced characteristics are then retrieved. In the end, a Multi-class with SVM is utilize to categorize the images into distinct categories. With this approach, apple fruit illnesses can be accurately detected and automatically classified, with up to 93% classification accuracy [26].

Pooling techniques for DNN are proposed by Gholamalinezhad & Khosravi(2020). These techniques are important for lowering dimensionality and computational complexity as well as enhancing model performance. This paper provides a comprehensive overview of the several pooling strategies applied to DNNs. It classifies and analyzes more modern inventions like global pooling with adaptive pooling techniques in addition to more established both average pooling and max. The impact of pooling algorithms on several network performance indicators like accuracy, recall, F1 score efficiency and robustness, is also examined in this work. This study seeks to further the field pertaining to deep learning by helping researchers and practitioners choose the right strategies for certain applications by providing an summary of the benefits and disadvantages of various pooling methods [27].

In Harakannanavar et.al.(2022) provides a thorough analysis of the detection of tomato Infections of the leaves of plants using ML and computer vision methods. In this approach there are several steps Firstly, resized the tomato leaves then use Histogram Equalization is utilized to enhance tomato sample quality's mean clustering done into enhances images in fist step for data space partitioning then contour tracing used to extract the border between the leaf samples in next step informative characteristics of the samples of leaves extract using various descriptors The GLCM with Transform of Discrete Wavelets. Finally, Classification has been done using Convolution CNN, KNN and SVM achieved accuracy 99.6%, 97% and 88% respectively [28].

Using the ImageNet dataset, the authors of He et al. (2016) evaluated deep residual networks (ResNets), reaching a depth of up to 152 layers, which is approximately eight times deeper than The VGG model networks but less complex. Using the ImageNet test set, a combination consisting of these ResNets obtains an error rate of 3.57%. The COCO object recognition dataset shows a 28% comparative improvement when using deep representations produced by ResNets [29].

In order to more effectively capture intricate interactions and dependencies among characteristics, the Ladder Capsule Network (LCN), as introduced by Jeong et al. (2019) Authors, combines the ladder network methodology with capsule networks. A reconstruction loss akin to that of ladder networks directs the routing mechanism amongst capsules placed hierarchically in the architecture. This methodology, which has been tested on multiple benchmark datasets, performs better than typical capsule networks, especially when handling complicated visual tasks. It also facilitates improved generalization and more effective utilization for the topological information in data. The findings demonstrate LCN's potential to further enhance capsule networks' capacities for a range of machine learning uses [30].

In Pradhan, P. et al. (2022). The authors proposed using digital images to improve advanced CNN models that have already been developed for the identification of apple diseases. Prominent CNN models, including InceptionV3, VGG16, ResNet50, DenseNet201, and DenseNet169, provided data that demonstrated their strong deep learning efficacy in differentiating between various apple diseases. At 98.75%, DenseNet201 achieved the highest accuracy, surpassing the other model [31].

In Khan & Narvekar (2022), Authors combines super pixel and color balancing approaches. The supplied image is initially converted into a color-balanced version to take uneven illumination into consideration. The modified image is then subjected to super pixel segmentation, which produces compact sections. To isolate the leaf image from the backdrop, an experimentally calculated threshold is applied to these super pixels' color channels and Histogram of Gradients (HOG). Then, photos with disease are identified K-means clustering is utilize. To depict sick areas, the method uses characteristics from GLCM in conjunction with the Pyramid of HOG (PHOG). Using Random Forest (RF), 93.12% accuracy was attained in the way illnesses are categorized [32].

In Khan et. al., (2023),Authors determine a node's trustworthiness, the suggested method uses a trust assessment model that incorporates a number of trust features, including social, indirect, and direct trust. Both Support Vector Machines as well as Random Forest are ML algorithms that are utilize to examine trust data and make conclusions about node activity and data integrity. Factors like Recall, Precision and F1-score are used to determine the system's performance and show how successfully it works to identify rogue nodes and provide safe data transmission [33].

Prior to classifying, the writers of Kurmi, Y. & Gangwar (2022) first located the leaf in the photos. By fusing, using color transformation and mapping algorithms on the leaf photos, they were able to extract valuable information. Following the extraction of the features, multilayer perceptron's, SVM and logistic regression were used to categorize. The accuracy of the finished model was 93.2% [34].

Color, texture, and form descriptors are among the features extracted from the limited leaf region in Kurmi et. Al.. (2021).A machine learning that classifies the various illness impacting the crop is then trained using these features. A collection of photos of leaves from various crops is used to assess the efficacy of the system, and the findings show that the approach performs well in classifying various diseases with high accuracy and robustness [35].

Shewale and Daruwala (2023) presented a method that can automatically extract features and classify illnesses in plants with high precision. This eliminates the requirement for threshold-based segmentation and manual feature engineering. Their expanded network is made to function with spatial images that are taken in difficult environmental circumstances. Recent advancements in the DL, area of computer vision have enabled the automation of disease recognition [36].

A four-step system was proposed by Adeel, A. et al. (2019). Enhancing the localized contrast underlying the symptoms with the neighbourhood contrasting haze reduction (LCHR) approach is the initial step. LAB colour transformation is used in the second phase, which chooses the optimal bandwidth based on image information. The third phase introduces noise as the form of redundant and irrelevant features, which are subsequently removed using Neighbour Component Analysis. Using a Multi-level SVM, fourth and last stage is classifying the reduced features. Using the grape leaf dataset, the suggested technique produced segmentation accuracy averages over 90% and classification accuracy values above 92% [37].

Manso et al. (2019) Utilized images involving coffee leaves to create an algorithm for detecting and categorizing foliar defects. During the segmentation stage, the study contrasted Otsu's algorithm, k-means, and iterative thresholding. The outcomes show how well the system works to automatically identify the severity degree of foliar damages and to detect and classify them .Fuzzy inference was used in the development of a smart phone application to identify agricultural diseases. Furthermore, a model of a deep neural net was applied to assess and categorize miner and rust of coffee leaf with over 97% accuracy in symptom categorization, allowing the determination of the severity of biotic stress [38].

Prajapati et al. (2017) describe a technique for recognizing and categorizing illnesses in the leaves of rice plants. Their methodology entails segmenting the afflicted areas using centroid-based K-means clustering, then extracting features from those areas by removing green pixels. After that, they use a SVM to categorize several classes, and on the training dataset, they obtain an accuracy of 93.33% [39].

In Rahman et al. (2021). For the need of improving breast cancer detection, the authors suggest an automated learning-based computer-aided diagnostic (CAD) system that combines clinical and anthropometric characteristics. To increase diagnosis precision, the approach makes use of both body measurements and information from medical histories. The suggested CAD system examines these several characteristics using cutting-edge machine learning algorithms to offer a more thorough evaluation of breast cancer risk [40].

Sharma, P. et al. (2020) introduced an AI-based method for automatically recognizing and categorizing plant illnesses. The process involves key procedures such gathering data, pre-processing, and segmentation and image classification. This AI-driven approach enhances plant productivity by streamlining disease detection [41].

Authors of Sannakki et.al. (2013) using image processing and AI methods to diagnosis illnesses in grape leaves. They start by feeding in images of grape leaves against intricate backgrounds. Anisotropic diffusion reduces noise and thresholding is used to mask green pixels. K-means is then utilized to divide the sick parts within the grape leaf to identifying them. Training a Back propagation neural network that is fed forward for categorization produced the most accurate results [42].

In Sethy et.al.(2020). Author applies transfer learning along with Convolution Neural Network architectures to group four distinct kinds of rice leaf diseases. Specifically, they mix a SVM with deep features taken from ResNet50 for classification. The outcomes were contrasted with those of conventional techniques, such as the use of SVM for patterns of local binary, the GLCM, and the histogram of directed gradients. With a 98.38% accuracy rate, the suggested strategy outperformed the conventional methods [43].

In Toseef(2018), Authors introduce mobile based fuzzy inference system where decision making engine work on back end for crop disease detection. This method is employed in decision-making and is closely related to the people of local language, as well as previous knowledge of crop disease. This technique can identify the primary diseases that affect Pakistan's two main crops, wheat and cotton. The suggested system's inference engine performed exceptionally well in predicting the correct illness, with up to 99% accuracy, when tested on an assortment of 100 genuine crop problems [44].

In Umamageswari & Irene (2023), Authors present a multi-step machine learning method for diagnosing plant illnesses. Preprocessing the images, which includes noise reduction and enhancement to increase image quality, is the process's initial stage. The Chameleon Swarm Algorithm (CSA) and Fuzzy C-Means (FCM) are combined to achieve segmentation in the second stage. Subsequently, the rapid Co-occurrence of Gray Levels The feature extraction process uses a matrix technique. Ultimately, Classification and identification of plant illnesses are achieved by the utilization of Progressive Neural Architecture Search (PNAS) [45].

In Upadhyay(2024),In order to anticipate which crops would be best for a given area, the authors of this work take into account of various data inputs, including soil quality, climate, and previous crop data. The technology uses sophisticated machine learning techniques to evaluate big datasets and produce precise crop suggestions. This strategy aims to improve crop yields, optimize farming methods, and advance sustainable farming. The paper highlights the system's ability to help farmers make educated decisions and uses experimental findings to demonstrate the system's efficacy [46].

In Upadhyay et al. (2024),In the framework of precision farming, the research introduces a unique machine learning approach intended to more accurately estimate crop yield. The project intends to increase the precision of yield predictions which are crucial for maximizing agricultural output and resource management by utilizing cutting-edge machine learning algorithms. In an effort to show how effective ML algorithms are at predicting crop output based on various agricultural data inputs, for this many machine learning algorithms are examined by the authors. Their application and performance indicators [47].

In Woo et al. (2018), Authors introduce CBAM which is readily integrated into convolution neural networks (CNNs) that are currently in use. To increase the network's capacity for representation, CBAM employs channel and attention to space modules in turn. By taking into account inter-channel interactions, the channel attention unit adapted recalibrates channel-wise feature responses, while the spatial attention module enhances spatial information by concentrating on significant areas within the feature map. Applying the suggested CBAM to different CNN architectures is simple, and benchmark dataset performance has improved significantly. Empirical findings reveal that CBAM continuously raises accuracy [48].

In Sunil, C. K. et al. (2023), Author introduced a Multilevel Feature Fusion Network (MFFN) for categorizing illnesses in tomato plants. The approach integrates ResNet50 and an Adaptive Attention Technique alongside MFFN, combining spatial, channel and pixel attention for improve classification accuracy. This method achieved a remarkable 99.88% training and validation accuracy on a large data set of pictures of tomato leaves [49].

In Zhou et al. (2015), Authors introduce a cucumber downy mildew detection system that makes use of the Support Vector Machine (SVM) classifications technique. They suggest a method that examines cucumber leaves and detects downy mildew symptoms by utilizing image processing techniques. The system's goal is to diagnose the disease accurately and reliably by employing the SVM classifier and collecting pertinent characteristics from leaf images. The outcomes show how well the SVM-based method separates healthy leaves from diseased leaves [50].

In Chung, H., and others (2019). The authors offer a novel method for approximating any random-utility choice model, which is a typical endogenous supply model that can be greatly enhanced through rescaling. It performed better than other similar models [51].

In Shahi, T. B. et al. (2023), Authors discussing a taxonomy that divides the crop illness estimation techniques employed into three categories in the literature. Major categories—ST, ML and DL-based investigation of meta-analysis previous works involving crop illness evaluation utilizing UAVs is carried out. We evaluate and compare the effects of UAV systems and sensors for agricultural disease estimation using such a comprehensive taxonomy, and traditional ML and DL techniques are employed for data analysis. The effectiveness of the ML and DL approaches is then discussed and contrasted with the conventional ST-based techniques for agricultural disease estimation employing UAVs. The analysis results show that while RGB sensors are chosen by DL algorithms, multispectral sensors are extensively used by ST and ML-based methods [52].

In Tulshan and Raul (2019), the authors outline the process of detecting plant leaf diseases, which includes pre-processing, segmentation, and the extraction of properties of the images. Once these steps are completed, they apply K Nearest Neighbour (KNN) classification for recognition and categorisation. The suggested model's remarkable accuracy of 98.56% in predicting plant leaf illness. Apart from illness prediction, the approach also highlights the affected area, sensitivity, and the duration of elapsed time [53].

2.1.3 Deep Learning Research related to Categorization and Identification of Plant Diseases

In Storey et al. (2022), the author's objective on identifying rust and leaf diseases in orchards of apples with Mask R-CNN with instance segmentation. They trained and evaluated R-CNN network backbones with three distinct Masks: MobileNetV3 and ResNet-50, implementing tasks such as object identification, segmentation, and disease detection. The ResNet-50-based Mask R-CNN model demonstrated high accuracy, particularly in identifying small lesions on leaves associated with rust disease. This study presents and evaluates a method for accurately detecting leaves and rust disease. It compares the performance of the three backbones, with the ResNet-50 backbone excelling at recognizing and segmenting very small objects, like rust spots on leaves. Meanwhile, the remaining backbones performed well in leaf recognition and division using MobileNetV3 standing out as a cost-effective solution for less powerful, CPU-based gadgets like smartphones. The use of labeled segmentation data provides a solid foundation for future research, with potential for dataset expansion through additional labeling efforts [54].

In Ullah, Z. et al. (2023), the authors suggested a hybrid model for deep learning combining Efficient-Net and Mobile-Net for recognizing and categorizing various tomato infections of plant leaves. This model, named EffiMob-Net, was developed by integrating the two models for deep learning and applying methods like dropout, regularization, and binarization to address over fitting. The final model effectively extracts characteristics from images of tomato leaves, achieving an impressive 99.92% of accuracy rate [55].

In Padilla, D. A. et al.(2020),Authors highlighted the importance of OpenMP in disease detection systems and Convolutional Neural Networks. These techniques are valuable for object identification and classification. The method achieved 93% accuracy in detecting Leaf Blight and 89% accuracy for Leaf Rust and Leaf Spot, using a corn leaf image dataset [56].

In Ahmed et al.(2023),Authors discuss about identifying and classifying harmful software is an essential cyber security task that aims to stop cyber threats. Machine learning along with transfer learning approaches can be used to adapt the Inception V3 approach, which is well-known for its effectiveness in identifying images tasks, for the classification of malware. A major development in cyber security is the Inception V3 technique, which uses machine learning with transfer learning to classify malware. This approach provides a highly accurate, scalable, and efficient way to recognize and classify malware by utilizing pre-trained models and deep learning. This methodology not only amplifies the capacity to detect and address cyber hazards but also augments the comprehensive efficacy of cyber security tactics [57].

In Ksibi, A. et al. (2022), Authors suggested a Deep Feature Concatenation (DFC) approach, which combines the features that were taken from two models for deep learning, ResNet50 and MobileNet. Using a large olive leaf image dataset collected through IoT based camera, their approach produced a remarkable level of precision of 97.08% [58].

In Arvind et al.(2021), Authors suggest a method plant disease classification has greatly benefited from the application pertaining to deep learning techniques, which have produced potent instruments for precise and automated disease diagnosis. By improving the decision-making process's transparency and comprehensibility, Explainable Artificial Intelligence (EAI) integration improves these methods. This method not only increases the accuracy of the classification but also offers practical suggestions for reducing illness two completely linked layers are positioned after three convolutions and three max pooling layers within this model. The outcomes of the investigation demonstrate the proposed model's superiority over previously models with training, like VGG16, MobileNet, and InceptionV3. The mean precision of the suggested model for nine classes of illness and one class of health is 91.2%. The accuracy of there are differences in the classification between 76% and 100% based on the class [59].

In Sabour et al.(2017),authors show that a multi-layer capsule network with discriminative training obtains outstanding results on the MNIST dataset and outperforms conventional convolution networks in identifying highly overlapping digits. An iterative routing-by-agreement method is responsible for this success, wherein a bottom-level capsule favors sending its results to higher-grade capsules with an active vectors possess a high scalar product utilizing the forecast of the lowermost capsule [60].

In Sharma, R. et al.(2020),Authors discuss that If paddy crop illnesses are not treated in their early stages, they can have a serious and deadly impact on the crops. For solving this issue they proposed deep learning model for prediction of paddy crop illness. With the use of CNN, the suggested model will enhance decision-making when dealing with a variety of diseases that affect rice crops, enabling early disease detection and preventing significant losses in yield output [61].

In Abbas et al.(2021), The authors describe a Conditional Generative Adversarial Network (C-GAN)- based on deep learning method for diagnosing tomato illnesses. They then train a Dense Network model using transfer learning using both synthetic as well as real images, allowing it to categorize images of tomato leaves into different illness groups. The precision of the suggested approach in classifying images of tomato leaves into five, seven, and ten groups was 99.5%, 98.6%, and 97.1%, respectively. [62].

In Singh & Arora (2020), Authors introduced a DCNN combined with transfer learning for recognise diseased and healthy wheat crops. They utilized different CNN methods, including AlexNet, VGG, and ResNet, to improve accuracy. The proposed algorithm ultimately achieved 98% accuracy in detecting wheat crop diseases [63].

In Shrivastava, V. K.et al. (2019), Authors introduced a DL technique called ResNext-MLP for identifying rice plant diseases. This method involves multi-level pre-processing, median filtering, and segmentation utilizing Fuzzy C-Means for pinpoint the affected areas of the rice plants. In their work, they utilized ResNext and a feature extractor to enhance performance, achieving an impressive accuracy of 98.89% [64].

In Ashwinkumar et al. (2022), the authors optimized a CNN based on MobileNet to create deep learning framework for the recognition of plant leaf illnesses. To determine the impacted regions of the leaf images, they used Kapur's thresholding technique for segmenting images and BF for preprocessing. Emperor penguin optimizer (EPO) was employed to maximize the parameters of the model after the MobileNet approach was employed to extract features. Ultimately, images of the leaves of the plants were classified with the correct class labels using a classifier from Extreme Learning Machines. This Mobile Net approach was achieved accuracy of 98.5% [65].

In Atila et al.(2021),With the aim of Plant leaf illnesses are categorized by authors that presented a DL framework based on Efficient Net and evaluated its effectiveness against other deep learning techniques. 55,448 plant images, including their augmented versions, were utilized for model training. The Efficient Net model's B4 and B5 variants demonstrated outstanding precision with rates of 99.39% as well as 98.42%, respectively, according to the results [66].

In Baser et al. (2023), Authors used a CNN to categorize tomato plant leaves into 10 distinct groups. They utilized a dataset that included 16,000 images of healthy and sick tomato leaves. The preprocessing stage reduced the image size, moreover, dataset was split for training and evaluation segments into 80:20 ratio. With an accuracy of 98.19%, the CNN architecture was composed of max pooling after four convolution layers [67].

In Bouguettaya et al. (2021), Authors examines new developments in the early identification of crop diseases using Unmanned Aerial Vehicles (UAVs) alongside deep learning techniques. The authors talk about the combination pertaining to deep learning algorithms that can analyze the images to identify early disease symptoms with UAV technology that provides high-resolution aerial imaging. Convolution neural networks (CNNs) along with additional sophisticated models are among the deep learning techniques covered in the review; their efficacy and possible uses in precision agriculture are highlighted. The research highlights how this combination improves crop tracking and disease control, enabling prompt actions to reduce crop losses [68].

In Chakravarthy et al. (2023), Authors provides a new method for balanced k-nearest neighbor (KNN) algorithm- based on deep learning meta-heuristic classification of breast cancer severity. The authors suggest an improved KNN method that optimizes the selection of neighbors by including Meta heuristic techniques, which increases the correctness of the model in determining the severity regarding breast cancer. In order to retrieve useful characteristics from medical data and apply them in the balanced KNN algorithm to provide accurate predictions, this approach uses pertaining to deep learning. According to the study, this method outperforms conventional techniques and presents a viable tool for the prompt diagnosis and severity classifying breast cancer [69].

In Deng & Yu (2014), Authors suggest that within the field of ML is deep learning. Which has made great strides and gained a lot of traction? This thorough analysis examines its methods and applications. An outline of core deep learning ideas, such as neural networks, training methods, and different designs including recurrent and convolution neural networks, is given by the writers. Additionally, they go over the use using deep learning across several domains like image processing, audio recognition, and NLP. The paper demonstrates how deep learning is an effective tool in contemporary artificial intelligence and signal processing because of its prowess in managing big datasets and intricate patterns [70].

In Elhassouny & Smarandache(2019),The authors of the study suggest a powerful deep CNN-model comprise of intelligent mobile application for identifying tomato leaf illnesses. This work, which can detect the 10 tomato leaf disease types that are most common, was motivated by the MobileNet CNN model for developing such type application. This model was developed using 7176 images of leaves from tomatoes, which were taught using a tomato leaf dataset. The smart mobile device uses these images to diagnose tomato diseases [71].

In Ertam & Aydın (2017), The MNIST dataset is frequently utilized in analysis of data studies—was classified using Tensor flow, which is among the most well-liked deep learning frameworks. The functions that are employed are sigmoid, soft plus, soft sign, tangent hyperbolic (Tanh), exponentially linear unit (eLu), and rectified linear unit (ReLu). Here, two learning-based ANN approaches are utilized such as SoftMax classifier and the CNN. The outcomes demonstrate that the ReLu activation technique yields the highest classification accuracy rate [72].

In Tiwari, V. et al. (2021), Authors introduce DL approach for identification and categorisation of various resolution images. In this work a vast gathering of plant leaf photos of several types is utilized for training an extensive CNN architecture. The proposed work considers 6 plants images of various categories under both in-lab and out-of-lab circumstances. This deep neural network has tackled several complicated and hard conditions associated with both intra-class and inter-class variances in images. To thoroughly assess the trained model across a range of parameters, cross-validations and testing on unobserved data are conducted. Experimental result achieved remarkable 99.58% accuracy of testing [73].

In Fraiwan et al. (2022), Authors suggest a method to categorizing of 3 corn. In this research, the authors provide deep transfer learning for diseases and healthy plants. This work does not require preprocessing because it uses a convolution neural network. Here, a range of situations for data splitting were used to conduct and extensively evaluate transfer learning. To prepare for variability in selecting random selections, this experiment was repeated 10 times. The performance of 98.6% was achieved for distinguishing the 4 classes [74].

In Gibert, D. et al. (2019), Authors discuss the visualization of malicious software while preserving its global structure, which aids in detecting variations. To achieve this, they proposed a DL approach that is file-agnostic for classifying different groups of malware software [75].

In Chellapandi, B. et al. (2021), Authors utilized several deep learning approaches, including VGG, ResNet, Inception, MobileNet, and DenseNet models, to detect diseases of plant leaves. They worked with 38 plant disease classification using transfer learning and plant disease types from the Plant Village Data Repository. Their method achieved an impressive 99% accuracy [76].

In Pouyanfar, S. et al. (2018), Authors investigated various DL methods and its application. In this investigation they concluded that Deep learning has become a rapidly developing technology that has been successfully used in many different fields and applications. Even though deep learning technologies are still being widely adopted in industry, cautious measures should be taken to guarantee that deep learning is applied appropriately. This is because models for deep learning that are subverted have the potential to cause considerable loss of money, trust, or in extreme circumstances, even human life [77].

In Jiang et al. (2019), Authors suggest a technique using deep for the immediate identification of illnesses of apple leaves. They employed the Google Net Inception architecture combined with Rainbow concatenation on a dataset of 26,377 augmented and annotated images of ill apple leaves. The model has been trained to identify five different apple leaf illness and achieved an accuracy of 78.80%, with a high processing speed of approximately 23.13 Frames per Second (FPS) [78].

2.1.4 Study of Hybrid Learning Model involved in order to Categorize and Identify Plant Diseases

Firstly, the authors in Jiang, F. et al. (2020) employ CNN to extract information from photos of rice leaf disease. The specific ailment is then classified and predicted using the Support Vector Machine technique. The hybrid model suggested by the 10-fold cross-validating approach achieved an accuracy rate of 96.8%, surpassing that of conventional approaches such as back propagation [79].

The authors of the article by Roy et al. (2023). Describe a Deep Convolution Network method for identifying illnesses of tomato leaves. They use a hybrid approach that combines a customized Deep Convolution Network built on PCA Deep Net with GAN with Approaches like Principal Component Analysis (PCA). Their remarkable accuracy rate of 99.60% is attained by using a Accelerated Region Convolution Neural Network (ARCNN) Architecture for identifying illnesses [80].

In Alshammari et al. (2022), the authors examined different types of olive diseases is crucial for preserving health and productivity of olive groves. Advanced machine learning methods, such as CNN and ViT can significantly enhance the effectiveness and accuracy of illness identification. Combined approach of CNNs and ViTs for classifying olive diseases marks a major technological developments in agriculture, offering a precise, efficient, and scalable solution for monitoring and managing the health of olive crops. This hybrid approach not only improves disease diagnosis but also supports more productive and sustainable olive farming practices. The study developed a hybrid DL model that integrates CNNs with ViT approach for classifying olive leaf diseases. The model was implemented for two and multiclass categorization. The results demonstrate the successful integration of CNNs with ViT models, achieving 96% accuracy in multi-class classification whereas 97% in binary classification. [81].

2.1.5 Study of Hyper Heuristic Approach

In plant disease detection, the hyper-heuristic technique is an enhanced optimization strategy that concentrates on choosing or creating appropriate heuristics to address a specific issue. Hyper-heuristics are capable of being used to optimize choosing features, algorithm selection, parameter tuning, and other detection system components in the framework of plant illness identification. This research articles provides below an overview of the employment of hyper heuristics in many fields.

In Pour et al. (2018), the authors designate the sub-regions that every member of the crew is accountable for while assigning sequence of repair jobs in Denmark to some crew members. When assigning responsibilities to crew members, there are two important factors to take into account. First and foremost, crew members' workloads need to be evenly distributed. Second, for the purpose of enable prompt response for the event of an unanticipated failure, the separation between two activities within a single sub-region must be minimized. They put forth influencing selecting hyper-heuristic framework that reassigns outliers using five different low-level heuristics for the purpose of improving original answers. Throughout a set using 12 benchmark issue instances, the findings of two hyper-heuristics are presented utilizing various initial solution creation techniques [82].

In Wall et al. (2018), Authors develop an evaluation methodology for interactive visualizations that is heuristic-based and used in conjunction with the value equation. All four value components are anagrammed to form the basis of the process known as ICET. Using this method, the four components are divided into recommendations, each of which consists of a tiny collection of basic heuristics. The visualization is subsequently evaluated in relation to the heuristics by evaluators who are familiar with visualization design concepts. Three interactive renderings of the identical data set were used for the methodology's first attempt, and each one was assessed by fifteen visualization specialists. It was discovered that the methodology yielded consistent ratings for all three visualizations and mirrored assessments of the visualizations' usefulness [83].

In Aron et al. (2015), Authors present techniques for grid computing that are not taken into account in conventional distributed computing settings. This effort aims to provide an effective method for safely allocating tasks to the right resources. An innovative hyper-heuristic resource scheduling technique based on swarm optimization for particle has been developed and applied to effectively plan tasks on the resources that are accessible while adhering to security protocols. The GridSim toolkit has been utilized to evaluate the efficiency of this algorithm [84].

In Barros et al. (2015), Author thoroughly examines the effects of various tactics to be applied as a fitness function in the process of evolution of a Hyper-Heuristic method for Evolution that generates decision-tree (HEAD-DT) induction algorithms automatically. They discuss about two different scenarios fist one is for balanced data sets to evolve a decision-tree and second one developing several unbalanced data sets to develop an algorithm for decision-tree induction. Here, experimental findings demonstrate that HEAD-DT outperforms the decision-tree inductive algorithms with statistical approach [85].

In Adriaensen et al. (2014), Authors discuss The Iterated Fair-Share Local Searching (IFSLS) hyper-heuristic, which is a recursive local search technique with a prudent restart condition. FS-ILS, a domain-independent version of the Metropolis condition, is used to select the heuristic in proportion with the level of acceptance of its previously suggested candidate solutions. This semi-automated design approach was established in previous work. Here, the authors concentrated more on the process of finding the method than the actual method [86].

In Asta & Özcan(2014),The authors discuss about hyper-heuristic method of searching or learning approach that combines many heuristic components or manages a collection utilizing simple heuristics develop heuristics for solving a particular computationally challenging task. a cutting-edge apprenticeship learning-based method that creates a hyper-heuristic enabling vehicle routing automatically. One could consider this approach to be a hyper-heuristic that employs a training and evaluation methodology [87].

In Alanazi & Lehre (2014), the authors discuss about how choosing the use of hyper-heuristics has effectively in a various type of problem domains. Because of their intricacy and random construction, Hyper-heuristics for selection are difficult to understand and interpret. Firstly examine the execution time of choosing hyper heuristics using a variety of widely used learning processes, including permutation, basic random, random gradient, and greedy. Using these learning mechanisms, the author derives the selection hyper heuristic's execution time on both a broad model of fitness landscapes and a classical example problem. Consequently, this aids in comprehending how hyper-heuristics behave. The findings indicate that the performance of all the hyper-heuristics taken into consideration is about equal [88].

In Grobler et al.(2015),The authors discuss the idea of heuristic space variety and look into several approaches to managing it in the framework of a metahyper-heuristic method in an effort to improve performance. Testing several approaches on a variety of floating point numbers benchmark problems reveals that hyper-heuristic performance is strongly influenced by the diversity of the heuristic space [89].

In Allen et al. (2013), Authors discuss the foundation for mass optimizing an aircraft's structural layout at the basic level of design is described in this paper by the authors that use a revolutionary hyper-heuristic technique. By encouraging solution search for space and reducing the chance of premature convergence, this hyper-heuristic approach improves the viability of and progresses toward the optimal solution discovered. [90].

In Asta et al.(2013),The authors examine the possible benefits and drawbacks of a hyper-heuristic that can handle a group of instances as a batch and finish them all in a single joint execution time, while allowing the hyper-heuristic to choose how to split the computational load among the individual instances. The author illustrates the large range of runtime variations that occur using the usual CHeSC benchmarks and provides evidence that suggests a batched mode may yield appreciable benefits [91].

In Vella et al. (2009), the authors address the growing usage of hyper-heuristics in combinatorial and function optimization. As opposed to attempting to solve The issue at hand with a fixed heuristic, a hyper-heuristic technique seeks out a collection of heuristics that collectively handle a problem that may then be immediately applicable to a group of issue instances. In data mining, hyper-heuristics have not received much attention. Author searches a space of decision- tree generation techniques using a hyper-heuristic method for data mining. A newly developed decision tree generation procedure is the outcome of this instance of hyper-heuristic search [92].

2.2 Research Gap Identification

After studying numerous literature reviews from various reputable journals and conferences on plant disease detection and classification, and examining various hyper-heuristic strategies, we have carefully reviewed the conclusion and future scope sections of these research papers. This comprehensive review has enabled us to determine the unexplored areas and research gaps in the domain. The identified research gaps are as follows:

1. Limited applications of filtering techniques along with deep learning model to extract the most significant features from images to improve the performance of plant leaf disease detection.
2. Many existing datasets are imbalanced which negatively impact the classification performance of plant disease detection model this give the scope of exploring class imbalance handling techniques like augmentation when deploying deep learning models.
3. There is limited research focuses on real time deployment of deep learning models for cucumber leaf disease detection in the field.
4. There is significant research scope for combining the strengths of different architectures to enhance the performance, accuracy and robustness of plant disease detection and classification.

5. Many of the researchers have used only one type of deep learning model for automatic feature extraction that may cause likelihood of missing significant features for plant leaf disease detection this give the scope of developing hybrid deep learning architecture for parallel feature extractions and combining these extracted features to reduces the likelihood of missing significant features.

2.3 Research Objectives

1. To Utilize the Gabor filter for texture feature extraction in plant disease detection.
2. To propose Deep Convolution Neural Network for identification of cucumber plant leaf diseases.
3. To introduce a transfer learning strategy to increase the precision of plant diseases identification and classification for small datasets.
4. To propose Hybrid deep learning model for further enhancement of plant leaf disease detection performance.

CHAPTER 3

DIAGNOSIS OF CUCUMBER DISEASES BY PLANT LEAVES USING A DEEPER CNN ARCHITECTURE

3.1 Introduction

The illness affects the plant's leaves because it obstructs photosynthesis. The primary disease of cucumber plants is powdery mildew, which usually appears in the initial and late phases of development. Many diseases, including Leaf spot on Alternaria, powdery and downy mildew, can damage the leaves of cucumber plants, which can hinder photosynthesis. Therefore, it's imperative to determine illnesses early on for the purpose of save plant life.

Owing to the extensive parameter requirements and costly calculations needed to alter traditional CNNs, The Pytorch package, that offers a vast array of DL techniques, was used in this work. A large number of four distinct kinds of both healthy and diseased leaves, along with certain parameters like batch size and time periods were contrasted. Various type of ML algorithms, including to evaluate the model's accuracy, self-organizing mapping, CNN, SVM, and the suggested approach are used. The proposed DCNN model produced better outcomes compared to the alternative techniques.

Authors of Sannakki et.al. (2013) use processing images and artificial intelligence techniques to diagnose illnesses in grape leaves. They start by feeding in images of grape leaves against intricate backgrounds. Anisotropic diffusion reduces noise and threshold is used to mask green pixels. Next, K-means clustering is employed to separate the sick parts within the grape leaf to identifying them. Teaching a Feed-forward neural network using backpropagation for categorization produced the most accurate results [42].

Wind and heat can exacerbate plant damage that has already occurred. Fruit that has the infection develops sunken, brown patches on its surface. The fruit may become brittle and powdery, and its colour may change from olive to black due to the lesions. If the contaminated fruit is not found until after harvest, problems with transportation or storage may result in monetary losses [6].

Downy mildew is one of the illnesses that Pseudoperonospora cubensis induces in cucumber leaves. A small yellow speck on the leafs upper surface is usually the first sign of the illness.

The disease eventually results in defoliation as these lesions grow and coalesce, turning the asymmetrical leaf margins brown. The undersides of the leaves of infected plants frequently display gray scale elements mold development Cantaloupes are not impacted by this disease, however it may lessen their taste. This pathogen prefers damp environments to grow. On the other hand, two fungus that colonize the upper surfaces of leaves, specifically Erysiphe cichoracearum and Podosphaera fuliginea cause powdery mildew. Plants that are infected may experience stunting, deformity, and early death. The fruits may not always be contaminated, but it can still negatively affect their size and growth [93].

This review focuses on two strategies for detecting plant diseases: methods based on volatile organic compound (VOC) profiling and methods utilizing spectroscopic imaging. Imaging with fluorescence and hyper spectral imaging are examples of spectroscopic imaging techniques, whereas VOC profiling-based detection examines volatile compounds emitted by both healthy and diseased plants using instruments such as electronic noses. The following are some examples of VOC profiling-based detection techniques: (i) background data interference; (ii) approach optimization for particular plants and diseases; and (iii) process automation for constant surveillance in real-world field circumstances [2].

Big data classification is made efficient with DL method. It needs a huge amount of tagged data for the suggested DCNN approach to train. But often, for the purpose of to develop a strong model, the given data may require to be more varied. The training data become more variable dataset grows larger in preprocessing like augmentation and transformation. By making use of the previously trained models. Acquired characteristics and weights, transfer learning may enhance performance in generalization and prevent over fitting. On the new dataset, the carefully selected ResNet model weights show the newly previously trained ResNet model performed better.

3.1.1 Technical overview

(i) Augmenting Data

Increasing the range of training information without gathering new data is possible through the use of data augmentation. In DL and ML method, this strategy is particularly useful for improving the performance and longevity of models by generating variations of existing data sets. PyTorch offers a versatile library with numerous techniques to facilitate data augmentation, enhancing model training by capturing relevant features. This method allows the model to distinguish between various networks classes by using data augmentation to highlight the most significant aspects [94].Several often employed augmentation methods listed below:

a) Rotation at Random: Rotates the image in an arbitrary degree range. Example: You can rotate an image left or right by up to thirty degrees. Arbitrary resized crop adjusts the image's size to a predetermined value and crops a random portion of it.

b) Combining Methods: Combining several augmentation methods to get data that is more varied. By increasing the diversity of the dataset, these strategies aid in representing the model and training it to distinguish between various classes.

(ii) Residual Network

Visual Geometry Group (VGG) created a deep CNN that comes in two variants: VGG16 as well as VGG19, named for their respective number of layers; GoogleNet, on the other hand, has extra layers in comparison to both. AlexNet makes eight layers combined with VGG where three completely connected layers using ReLU activation and five max-pooling layers on top.In deep networks, the problem of vanishing gradient presents the significant challenge for training models. When gradients are repeatedly multiplied, they become very small, leading to performance saturation or a sharp decline. The residual network (ResNet 50) tackles this issue by utilizing millions of convolutional layers, outperforming shallower networks in addressing problem of vanishing gradient. The complexity of network is further enhanced by adding additional layers to more accurately capture features. [29].

The mapping is fitted by stacking nonlinear layers described in Equation 3.1, with the original mapping recast into Equation 3.2. The operational diagram of the network of residuals is displayed in Figure 3.1.

$$F(X) = Y(X) - X \tag{3.1}$$

$$F(X) = Y(X) + X \tag{3.2}$$

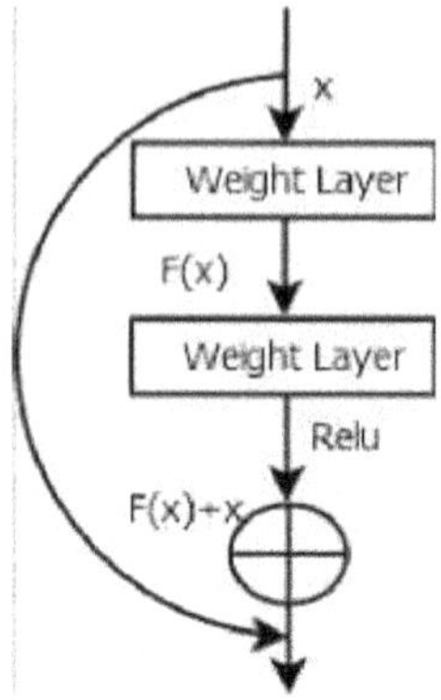

Figure 3.1 Residual network working diagram

Deeper neural networks require more complex training methods for images datasets. Residual networks use neural networks to get around the challenge of training datasets. If the resolution of every layer—previous, output, and subsequent—is precisely the same, the filter gets deeper. Consequently, when the depth doubles, the map of features only goes half the depth.

(iii) Convolution neural networks (CNN)

Convolution neural networks require less preprocessing than other classification methods with sufficient training because they primarily consist of Three layers: totally linked, pooled, and convolution. These layers construct the metaphysical duo an image collection. CNN can retrieve images information and learn filters. Superior performance when it comes to picture and audio signal inputs can effectively cover the whole region. Convolution networks are distinct from other neural networks because of this [94].

3.2 Related work

It's challenging to accurately convey the complex shape and consistency of a leaf in plant leaf categorization when using traditional methods. CNN are advantageous for classifying plant leaves due to robust feature extraction and classification capabilities. Here, a CNN with ten layers was built to categorize plant leaves. The photos were enhanced with patterns to increase the categorization and broaden the dataset. Visualization was used to analyse the factors affecting accuracy. By utilizing CNN, the Leaf Collection Flavia, consisting of 4,800 leaf images from 32 different species, attained a remarkable level of accuracy 87.92% [95].

In Ertam & Aydın (2017), MNIST dataset—which is highly used in analysis of data studies—was classified using Tensor flow, which is among the most well-liked deep learning frameworks. The functions that are employed are sigmoid, soft plus, soft sign, tangent hyperbolic (Tanh), Exponentially Linear Unit (ELU), and Rectified Linear Unit (ReLu). Here, two learning-based ANN are utilized: SoftMax classifier and the Convolution Neural Network (CNN). The outcomes demonstrate that the ReLu activation technique yields the highest classification accuracy rate [72].

Tomato plants illness recognition model was developed by De Luna et al. (2018). To diagnose leaf diseases, they designed a motorized image capture box that took images from all every tomato plant's four sides. The tomato variety used for the experiment was Diamante Max. CNN were applied to analyse the images and identify the diseases. Transfer Learning-based illness recognition model achieved an accuracy rate of 95.75%, while F-RCNN model for detecting anomalies produced an accuracy of 80%. Using the automated image capture system, tomato leaf diseases were identified with a 91.67% accuracy rate [95].

A suggested CNN model for effective distinguishing plant illness; a group of photos illustrating healthy and unhealthy plants was gathered using different accessible sources and manually; the trained CNN model has been evaluated and confirmed to have high precision under field conditions. Generally, humans are able to recognize plants that suffer from specific illnesses, ability to see, it's more difficult to identify them. Beyond prompt care and swift action, every plant in the farming area may become diseased, resulting for circulate of disease to surrounding plants [1].

In Prakash et al. (2017), Suggest GLCM was used for the purpose of extract features and classification using SVM and K-Mean Clustering for segmentation for the purpose of recognize and categorize illnesses on leaves. Model's accuracy was 90% as a result of this strategy [15]. In Phadikar & Sil. (2008), zooming is utilized to extract image data. RGB spots have been recognized with 92% accuracy using a map that self-organized with a neural network to identify rice disease [12].

In Pooja et al. (2017), Diseases are detected and categorized using image processing along with DL methods. SVM is utilized for identifying the images, obtaining a 92.4% rate of accuracy [13].

In Nashrullah (2021). Presented an algorithm for detecting illnesses on tomato leaves with an accuracy of 90.37%. Preprocessing the dataset, segmenting it, extracting features, classifying it, and assessing its performance were all parts in the process. The textural properties of the tomato leaves were analyzed using both color-based and Gabor filters [11].

The model that Zhou et al. (2015) developed makes use of SVM classification. Following picture processing, the SVM effectively identified three varieties of cucumber diseases: leaf Powdery, downy, and rusty mildew, with an accuracy of 90% when determining the state of the leaves [50].

Khan et al. (2020) developed an algorithm for recognizing and categorizing cucumber leaf diseases by segmenting the affected areas, enhancing the images, and performing feature extraction and selection for classification. They introduced a novel segmentation technique called Sharif Saliency-Based (SHSB), combined with fusion for the purpose of extract features, they utilized models that have already been trained VGG-M and VGG-19. Ultimately, SVM was employed to detect five different cucumber leaf diseases, achieving an accuracy of 98.08% in just 10.52 seconds [143].

Ma and colleagues (2018), created a deep neural network that uses convolution layers to detect four different kinds of cucumber illness: Anthracnose, powdery and downy mildew with leaf spots target achieved 93.4% accuracy rate. Additionally, they contrasted the DCNN's performance with that of other classifiers [146].

Atila and colleagues (2021), Authors presented the architecture of EfficientNetB0. It was trained using 61,486 pictures taken from the supplemented dataset and 55,448 photos from the original dataset. Incredible accuracy with rates of 99.91% as well as 99.97% was attained by this method [66].

In Shoaib and colleagues (2022), the authors focused on tomato leaves and classified six different tomato leaf diseases using the InceptionNet along with Modified U-Net techniques. The accuracy rates of their models were 99.12% and 98.73%, respectively [138].

In 2017, Sengür and colleagues presented an approach for segmenting the retinal vascular system. With an accuracy of 91.78%, this model detects retinal arteries using two layers of convolution, one loss level, single dropout layer, and two pooling layers [139].

Alshammari and colleagues (2022) used 3,400 phtos of different Olive leaves for training a model they constructed to determine the most useful attributes. VGG-16, VGG-19, and ViT are three deep learning algorithms were utilized to compare the outcomes. With an accuracy of 97%, their hybrid approach which combines the ViT approach with the VGG-15 model performed the best out of all of them [81].

In Kumar and Janet (2022), the technique, called Deep Transfer Malware Image Classification (DTMIC), uses pre-trained CNN to apply transfer learning to categorize photos into several malware families after converting malware binaries into grayscale images. In comparison to conventional malware classification techniques, the model demonstrated good performance and accuracy metrics after being instructed and assessed on a sizable dataset of malware images. The suggested DTMIC offers an expandable answer for real-world cyber security issues by employing transfer learning to significantly reduce the amount of time spent training while preserving robustness and accuracy in identifying and categorizing malware kinds [148].

The authors of Esgario et al. (2020) suggested CNN-based multi-task approach. They also looked into using data augmentation methods to enhance the precision and resilience of the system. In computational trials, the suggested system utilizing the ResNet50 model achieved an accuracy rate 86.51% for estimating the intensity of biotic stress and 95.24% for classifying it. Furthermore, it was discovered that the results were higher that 97% when the symptoms were the only thing classified [149].

The CNN method and the Vision Transformer (ViT) were presented by Borhani et al. for the categorization of illnesses in the Wheat Rust and Rice Leaf datasets. According to their research, models with convolutional and attention blocks combined offered higher accuracy [4].

Table 3.1 provides a summary of the relevant work that has been discussed.

Related work	Methodology
Liu and colleagues (2018)and Hari and colleagues (2019)	Construct a CNN
Jiang and colleagues(2019)	Rainbow Concatenation Method with Google Neural Network
Ertam & Aydın (2017)	Comparison of the hyperbolic tangent (tanH), sigmoid, soft plus, and rectified linear unit (ReLu).
De Luna and colleagues (2018)	Method of transfer learning
Prakash and colleagues (2017)	K Mean Clustering, SVM, and GLCM
Phadikar & Sil (2008)	An autonomous map utilizing a neural network
Pooja and colleagues (2017)	Deep learning methods and image processing
Nashrullah and colleagues (2021)	Gabor filters
Zhou and colleagues (2015)	SVM
Khan et al. and colleagues(2020)	Selection of deep features methodology
Ma et al., (2018)	Deep convolutional neural networks are compared to SVM and random forests.
Atila and colleagues (2021)	EfficientNetB0
Şengür and colleagues(2017)	Modified U-Net and InceptionNet methods
Shoaib and colleagues (2022)	VGG-16
Alshammari and colleagues (2022) and Borhani and colleagues (2022)	ViT and CNN methodology

Table 3.1 Enumerates the salient characteristics that set the reviewed study apart.

3.3 Methods and Materials

Convolution neural networks (CNNs) are used to detect cucumber leaf illness by training a model to categorize images of cucumber leaves into several disease groups. Because CNNs can automatically train to detect features like edges, textures in particular, and shapes using the input images, they are useful for image classification applications. Figure 3.2 representing the work flow diagram of detection of cucumber plant leaf illness by using CNN.

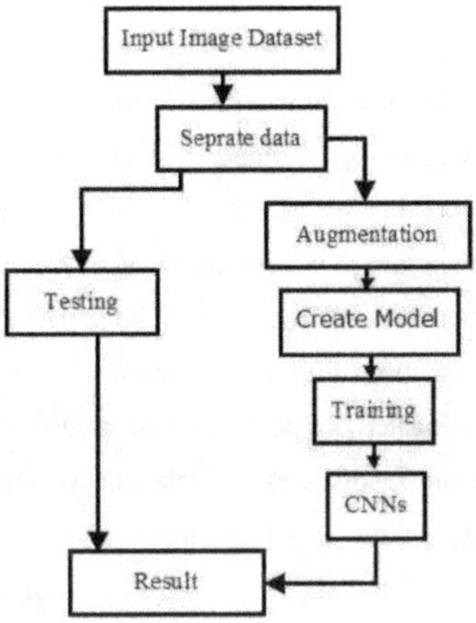

Figure 3.2 Work Flow Diagram [137]

3.3.1 Proposed approach

The suggested approach for identifying cucumber leaf illness is depicted in the block diagram. Collecting datasets, enhancing data, building models, training, validation and classifying them are important elements. The recommended model architecture and process flow are presented in Figure 3.3.

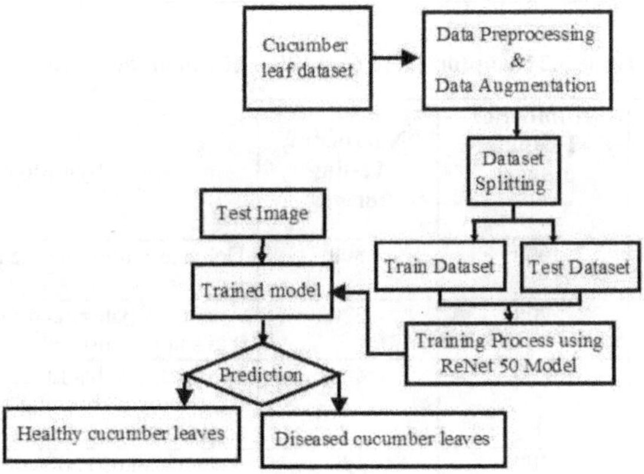

Figure 3.3 Recommended Model Architecture

3.3.2 Data set description

This study necessitates a large image dataset to instruct the model effectively, ensuring accurate predictions. Figure 3.4 showcases 3,700 images of cucumber leaves, encompassing four Categories include healthy cucumber leaves, Alternaria leaf spot, powdery mildew, and downy mildew. Table 3.3 details the amount of images used in assessment and training, along with the symptoms of various cucumber diseases from Plant Village. Here 67% of dataset is designated for learning and 33% for validation. Figure 3.4 presents number of images utilized in the research, as well as those allocated for learning and assessment. Additionally, Table 3.2 outlines the symptoms of cucumber diseases and relevant weather conditions. The symptoms and appearance of these diseases are covered in Chapter 1, specifically in Section 1.4.

Type of Cucumber Illness	Symptoms	Conditions
Downy mildew	Yellowing diseased leaves have the potential to fall down the tree.	Lot of moisture in the soil and regular rainfall.
Powdery mildew	Wherever the illness is present, dark, brittle patches emerge, indicating the approaching mortality and defoliation.	Dry and cold.
Alternaria leaf blight	On the oldest leaves, little brown specks encircled by an aura of yellow may indicate a number of plant illnesses and environmental variables.	The last of spring's shadows and first sunny summer days

Table 3.2 Symptoms and Condition of Cucumber Diseases

Categories of illnesses	Number of Training Images	Number of Testing Images	Symptoms
Powdery mildew	600	300	Delicate white and Leaf, pale yellow patches.
Downy mildew	700	320	Angles of pale green to yellow on the leaf's upper surface.
Alternaria leaf spot	800	400	Leaf patches that range from yellow to dark brown become black, with a focused target circles.
Healthy	400	180	No such signs and symptoms.

Table 3.3 Explanations of various cucumber sicknesses

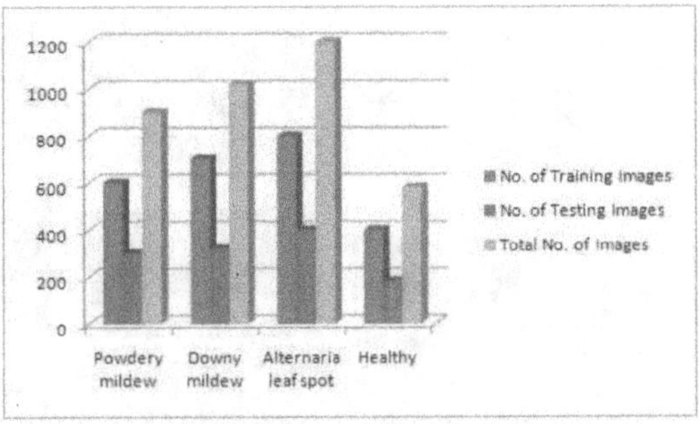

Figure 3.4 Total amount of images snapped for the task completed divided by the amount of distinct picture data in the learning and assessment data sets

3.3.3 Data Enhancement

The training set of 3,700 images is improved by the proposed work using three different data augmentation techniques: Random Rotation, Random Adjusted Crop, and an integration of both. Every image is rotated by a random angle of as much as thirty degrees towards the left or right using the Random Rotation technique. The Random Adjusted Crop technique preserves a preset aspect ratio by randomly resizing each image within 0.07 to 1.0 of its initial dimension. Cropping the photos using the center-cropping approach is the second step. The third way combines the preceding two approaches using the compose function, enabling the sequential application of numerous modifications. Data augmentation values, sample images of healthy and ill cucumber leaves, and examples of augmented Downy mildew leaf images are shown in Figure 3.5, Table 3.4 shows Augmentation approach of images and Figure 3.6 shows sample augmentation result of Downy mildew.

Augmentation approach	Values
Zooming	30%
Rotation of image	30
Horizontal Flipping of Image	True

Table 3.4 Values for augmented data that are employed in these methods

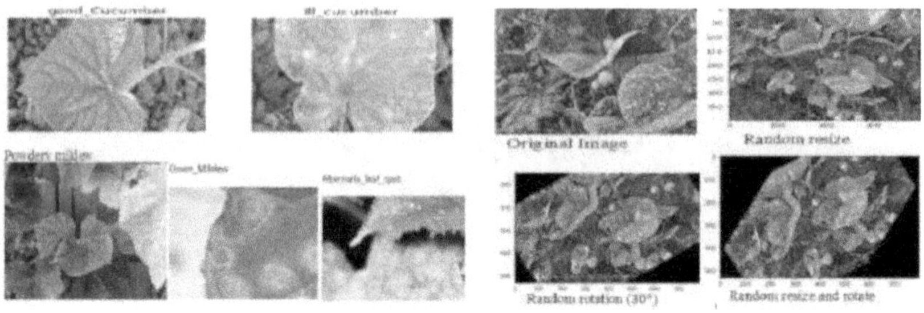

Figure 3.5 Image of healthy, unhealthy cucumber leaves and augmented downy mildew leaves

3.3.4 Transfer Learning

Transfer learning paradigm is applied to CNNs in two phases using the trained ResNet-50 model while fixed feature extraction is used in the second phase, the CNN is first adjusted based on predetermined parameters. To use a feature extractor strategy, the CNN's default settings, which include those in the last layer—are kept intact. The integration of ResNet-50 with images collections looks like this: The first step is to introduce pre-trained model.

For the purpose of match the number of subclasses within our collection, the fully interconnected final layers in the ResNet-50 framework are changed and swapped out for six fully interconnected Soft-Max layers. Convolution layers have set weights and specifications. The approach is capable of identifying a range of illnesses in cucumbers.

An optimization technique is utilize to evaluate all of the parameters during training. One very powerful deep learning technique is Transfer learning, which lets you employ previously trained models for new tasks. By utilizing a neural network trained on hundreds of images, pre-trained models improve performance. The ResNet-50 model uses the included image datasets to extract features like corners, boundaries, and curves for image classification. The block at the bottleneck completes the extraction of features phase, leaving simply the categorizing phase. The framework's completely interconnected bottom layers are modified to meet our classification needs; this ensures that the biases, weight and other hyper parameters remain unchanged upon import of the model [96].

3.3.5 ResNet-50 Architecture

A three-layer stack of 50 neural network layers makes up the ResNet-50 architecture. Its accuracy is higher than ResNet-34. 3x3 convolutions are utilize in design, and for nonlinearity, ReLU activation and batch normalization come next. The convolutions minimize the spatial dimension among the feature maps in half and increase amount of channels by two at each level. Pooling global averages is used to provide the outcome of categorizing. ResNet-50 is comparatively lightweight in comparison to other networks of its kind, with 23.5 million parameters and 3.8 billion FLOPs. Skip connections are used by ResNet-50 to attach the resultant layers [147]. The architectural schematic of ResNet-50 is depicted in Figure 3.6 and the architecture with and without skip connections are as illustrated in Figures 3.7(a) and 3.7(b).

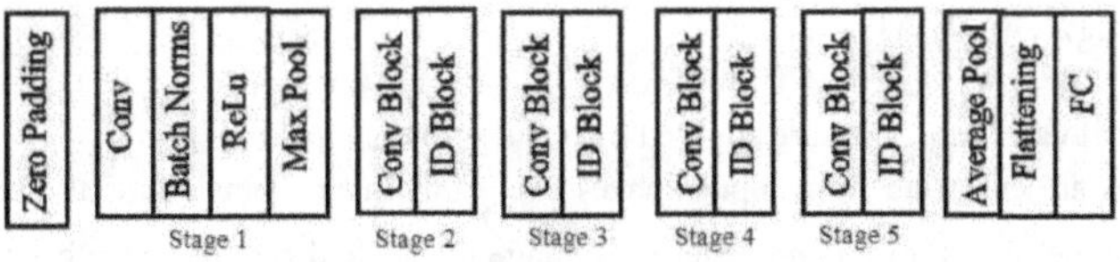

Figure 3.6 Architecture of Resnet-50

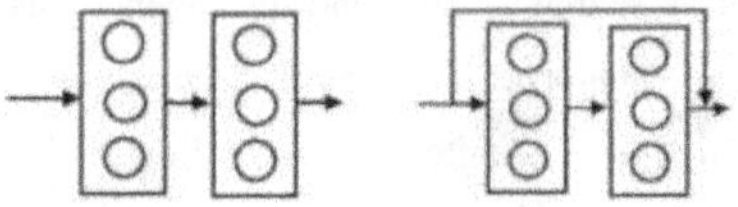

Figure 3.7 (a) and 3.7 (b) Both with and without a skip connection

ResNet50's residual learning technique, which successfully addresses the vanishing gradient issue typical of deep architectures, is the main reason it beats other deep neural network models for cucumber disease diagnosis. Because of this, ResNet50 is better than traditional CNNs at capturing fine-grained textural differences in cucumber leaves, such as vein patterns, lesion borders, and subtle discolorations, even as the level of the network increases. Even with a moderate dataset size, the usage of skip connections guarantees effective gradient flow and speeds up convergence throughout training, making it resistant to overfitting.

Additionally, robust feature generalization is provided by ResNet50's pretrained ImageNet weights, which adapt well to agricultural picture domains when refined through transfer learning. ResNet50 strikes a better mix between computational economy and representational capacity than models like VGG19 and InceptionV3, which results in improved classification accuracy and shorter training times for datasets related to cucumber leaf disease.

3.3.6 ResNet-50 Layers

ResNet-50 was introduced by Microsoft Research. 50-layer deep convolution neural network model, in 2015. It has performance in semantic segmentation, image categorization and object recognition. Below is a description of the layers that comprise the architecture:

(i) Convolution Layer:

If matrix A contains two variables, x and y, the convolution matrix $C_{x,y}$ as indicated in Equation 3.3, is computed.

$$C_{x,y} = \sum_u \sum_v a_{u,v} b_{x-u+1,y-v+1} \quad (3.3)$$

Where all valid subscripts are covered by u and v for $a_{u,v}$ and $b_{x-u+1,y-v+1}$
Features are extracted from input images using this layer. It maintains the relationships between the pixels. In this procedure, an image matrix and filtering have been employed. A well-known deep convolution neural networks model with 50 layers is called ResNet-50. It was unveiled by Microsoft Research in 2015, and since then, it has demonstrated cutting-edge capabilities in image categorization, object recognition, and segmentation of semantics. The ResNet-50 high-level architecture is as follows:

(ii) RELU Layer

An input's nonlinearity is increased by the Rectified Linear Unit (RELU) layer.

(iii) Pooling Layer

A single neuron contains all of the data from the preceding layer thanks to pooling layers. The maximum element in a 2x2 feature map is chosen by this model via max pooling.

(iv) Flatten Layer

One direction continuous layer is created using pooling layer's data. via the flattening layer.

(v) Fully Connected Layer

Convolution layer's output is delivered to the resulting layer after being flattened. The fully linked layer carries out learning with nonlinear feature combinations. Figure 3.9 shows the framework of the fully linked layer.

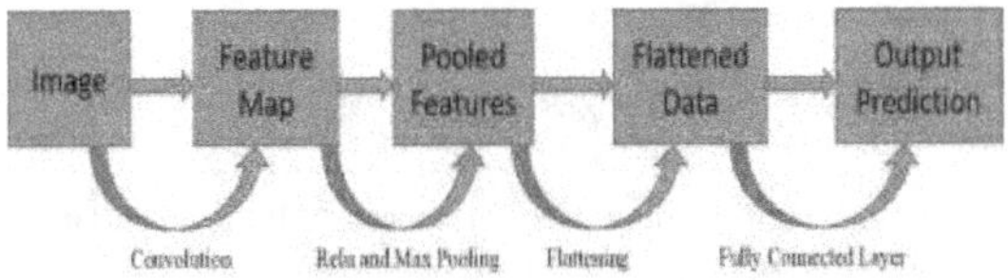

Figure 3.8 Fully Connected Layers

3.3.7 Softmax Function

An activation function called the softmax function is employed to forecast a problem's probability distribution. It is frequently used to guarantee membership over more than two class labels in multiclass classification tasks.

3.3.8 Training and Validation

Instead of explicitly predicting the intended underlying mappings, residual networks, or ResNets, are made for training residual functions with respect to input layers through learning residual mappings. This method improves system performance while streamlining model optimization. Previous blocks are stacked in these networks to increase functionality. The research finds that the hybrid residual-dense structure, which combines several dense layers with residual networks, efficiently categorizes images for the purpose of analyzing leaf diseases.

For the purpose of recognize and classify diseases, ResNet50 lacks dense layers and instead uses convolutional layers. Eight by eight pixel images and fixed batch dimensions of forty are used. New layers are created by training six fully connected layers. Training is done across 50 epochs, with active gradients from earlier layers being back propagated and model weights updated via the Adam optimizer.

Classification Using CNN: Image categorization based on CNN is frequently used in DL investigations. Here, CNN are used to process 2D pictures through filters for hidden layers, input and response for the purpose of provide a class and label to an image. Convolution, The completely connected layers, pooling, and ReLU are examples of hidden layers that have a big influence on CNN image processing and classification. Utilizing the probability distribution function is determine the proper class using the softmax function. Negative values are regarded and as for this, positive exponential is employed. Equation 3.4 illustrates the likelihood of this specific kind.

$$\sigma(X)_i = \frac{e^{X_i}}{\sum_{j=1}^{N} e^{X_j}} \text{ for } i = 1, \ldots, N \text{ and } X = (X_1, \ldots\ldots, X_N) \tag{3.4}$$

Here N indicate the total amount of categories for specific illnesses, and the input value is Xi.

3.4 Results and Conversation

A data augmentation strategy is used to optimize the training procedure and raise the precision of the model without obtaining more datasets. This procedure entails expanding the dataset with additional Images. In the event of a loss during training the model's parameters are updated through the use of back propagation of the gradient. To categorize images into multiple categories, a deep CNN that has received prior training on a big dataset is used, called ResNet-50. A likelihood distribution that shows the chance of a picture input falling into every class is ResNet-50's output. The results of the ResNet-50 are changed to a probability distribution between 0 and 1 with the softmax function. Input value of softmax functions can be changed to convert a probability distribution using the ResNet-50 output rate. While training proceeds more slowly with a lower learning rate value, overall performance improves. Adam, the optimizer of the PyTorch library, was used in this trial, and his 0.001 as the default learning rate was applied. The log-probabilities for each class are compared to the goal values in Equation 3.5. The output is chosen to be the value that is predicted with the highest probability. 'p' stands for the expected values for a specific model and 'q' for the consequent values in this equation

$$.\log(p, q) = -\log q \tag{3.5}$$

This section outlines the setup for the experiment and performance analysis of the suggested method for diagnosing and classifying cucumber plant diseases. It outlines the experimental environment, including hardware specifications, software details, and the training and validation datasets. Two trials are conducted: one for without augmentation and another for with augmentation. The section also covers the training and validation processes for both approaches, a comparison of their results, and a final comparison between the suggested approach and previous studies. The discussion is organized into five subsections.

3.4.1 Experimental environment

Dataset with images of cucumber leaves is acquired via plant village dataset. There are three In addition to one group of healthy leaves, this dataset contains three kinds of sick leaves. We have performed research on this dataset, two experiments for the two approaches: the first experiment is related to the application of deep CNN architecture without augmentation from input samples, and the second experiment deals with the application of deep CNN architecture with augmentation from input samples using transfer learning technique. In order to validate the model, The dataset is split 80:20 divisions, with 80 percent being used for training and 20 % for testing. All of the experiments are run on a Lenovo laptop features a 1.80 GHz Core i5 CPU. The laptop mentioned above has 250 GB of SSD and 4 GB of DDRAM. This laptop is equipped with Windows 10 OS. In implementation, all the experiments are performed in Python using colab. Tensor Flow and PyTorch libraries are utilize in Python implementation of the suggested deep convolution neural network (DCNN) model. The model's performance is assessed using the Plant Village repository's cucumber leaf dataset.

3.4.2 Observation of training-validation of approach 1

Original data was fed into the proposed deep CNN model in order to conduct Experiment 1. The classification performance of the suggested model for method 1 has been assessed here. Table 3.3 lists the training-validation samples that were utilized to experiment with the model's initial training and validation. There were 100 iterations in each of the 12 epochs we used. In order to observe the outcomes of strategy 1 (experiment 1), 1200 iterations were carried out. Training process and Validation steps are depicted in Figure 3.9. Here, Figure 3.9 depicts model's accuracy and loss vs. the number of epochs during training-validation process. A The model's efficacy is demonstrated using a confusion matrix. Figure 3.10 uses a confusion matrix to show the correct and incorrect classifications of the proposed model for method 1. The general precision of the developed system is indicated in Table. 3.5.

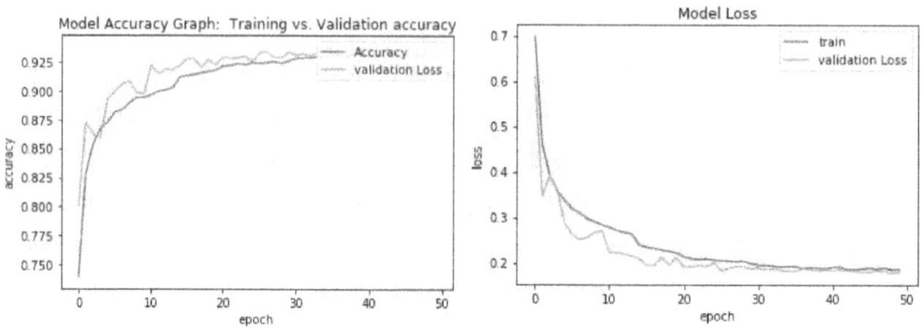

Figure 3.9 Model accuracy and loss before augmentation

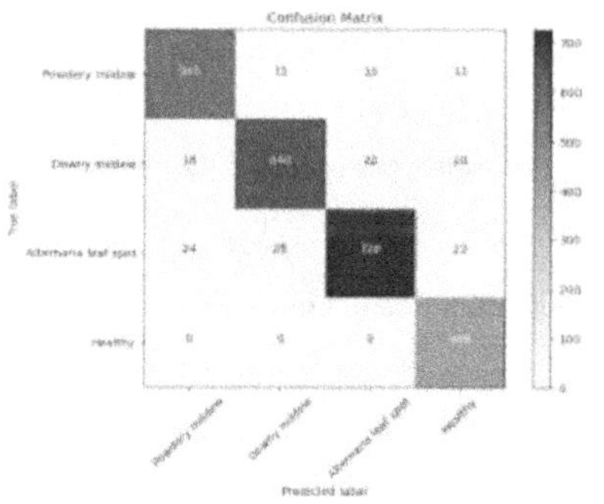

Figure 3.10 Confusion matrix before augmentation

Leaf illness	Healthy	Powdery Mildew	Alternaria leaf spot	Downy Mildew	% of Accuracy
Powdery Mildew	11	565	13	11	94.2%
Downy Mildew	20	18	22	640	91.4%
Alternaria leaf spot	22	24	726	28	90.8%
Healthy	400	0	0	0	100%
	Average	**94.1%**			

Table 3.5 Confusion matrix for each of the three classes prior to data augmentation

3.4.3 Observation of training-validation of approach 2

The developed deep CNN architecture is utilized in approach 2(experiment 2) using a pre-processed dataset. Data augmentation from each and every sample image to enhancement of data from the cucumber leaf picture, transfer learning method proposed by ReNet. The suggested model's classification results for approach 2 were examined in this section. The processed dataset with the same validation and training division as displayed in Table 3.3 utilized for training and verify the suggested model. The same number of epochs, in addition to the same quantity of iterations per epoch as discussed in approach 1, is used to provide learning to the suggested system. Both studies use the same training and validation setup. The validation and training accuracy and loss of the suggested system for approach 2 during the validation and training procedure is shown in Figure 3.11.With the use of a confusion matrix, right and wrong predictions of the suggested deep CNN architecture for approach 2 have displayed in Figure. 3.12. The augmented images improves the learning ability of the suggested model, resulting in an increase in accuracy from 94.1 percent to 98 percent and a decrease in the loss with the equivalent proportion. Overall accuracy shown in Table 3.6. The loss incurred following every iteration and validation determines number of epochs are utilized to instruct the model. Equation 4 shows the negative NL Loss functional by which the loss can be predicted with log-likelihood, where 'q' is the predicted value and 'p' is the response. The accuracy for cucumber leaf disease is predicted by the confusion matrix both prior to and following data augmentation. Depending on the augmentation used both before and after, Tables 3.5 and 3.6 display Overall precision of several diseases, including leaf spot on Alternaria, powdery mildew, and downy mildew. The training model assessed greater accuracy, which decreased the loss, and the suggested CDD model covered a wide region. Figures 3.10 and 3.12 display confusion matrix both prior to and following augmentation. Figures 3.9 display the model accuracy and loss prior to augmentation and Figures 3.11 displays the model accuracy and loss following augmentation. It is evident that the loss stabilizes after thirty epochs.

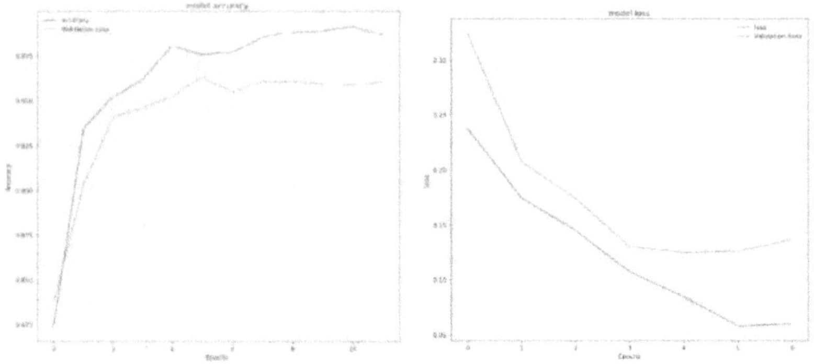

Figure 3.11 Model accuracy and loss after augmentation

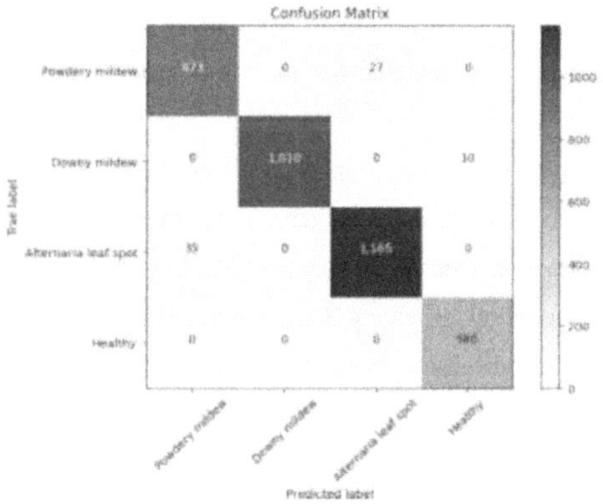

Figure 3.12 Confusion matrix after augmentation

Leaf illness	Healthy	Powdery Mildew	Alternaria leaf spot	Downy Mildew	% of Accuracy
Powdery Mildew	6	580	8	6	96.7%
Downy Mildew	6	4	6	684	97.9%
Alternaria leaf spot	6	10	774	10	97.5%
Healthy	400	0	0	0	100%
Average		**98.0%**			

Table 3.6 Confusion matrix for each of the three classes following data augmentation

Additional Context and Analysis

In addition to overall accuracy, class-wise performance indicators like recall, precision, and F1-score can be displayed to give a more thorough picture of the model's behavior. These measures emphasize the model's advantages and disadvantages and provide a better understanding of how it functions across various disease categories.

Table 3.7 Metrics for Class-wise Performance

Class	**Precision (%)**	**Recall (%)**	**F1-Score (%)**
Powdery Mildew	96.4	96.7	96.6
Alternaria Leaf Spot	97.0	97.5	97.2
Downy Mildew	97.5	97.9	97.7
Healthy	100.0	100.0	100.0
Average	**97.7**	**98.0**	**97.9**

The recall levels show the model's capacity to identify all pertinent cases of a specific condition, whereas the accuracy values for each category show the proportion of correctly detected positive predictions. A balanced indicator of the model's overall accuracy is the F1-score, which is the harmonic mean of precision and recall.

A deeper look at the confusion matrix (Figures 3.12 and 3.15) reveals that the majority of misclassifications happen between illnesses that have similar visual traits, including downy mildew and powdery mildew. This suggests that even though the model's overall accuracy is great, it occasionally has trouble differentiating between diseases that have almost identical symptoms. It would be easier to understand the underlying causes of such errors—such as differences in lighting, background interference, or partial visibility of infected regions—if visual samples of these incorrectly classified photos were presented.

3.4.4 Performance analysis between approach 1 and approach 2

An effective diagnostic tool that offers thorough evaluation of an assessment the effectiveness of the model is the ROC curve. When adjusting model limitations, comparing models, and assessing performance on unbalanced datasets, it facilitates better decision-making by visualizing the consequences of choosing among true positive outcomes and frequency of false positives. Figures 3.13 show the Receiver Operating Characteristics curve (ROC curve), it shows the model's efficacy both before and after augmentation. Plotting positives of false and true is one method of validating the performance of the model assessment. The suggested model's curve, shown in Figure 3.13, outperforms the prior data enhancement curve, based on the ROC plot. This suggests that the suggested model has a greater the region beneath the curve, showing better categorization, and correctly predicts all major diseases.

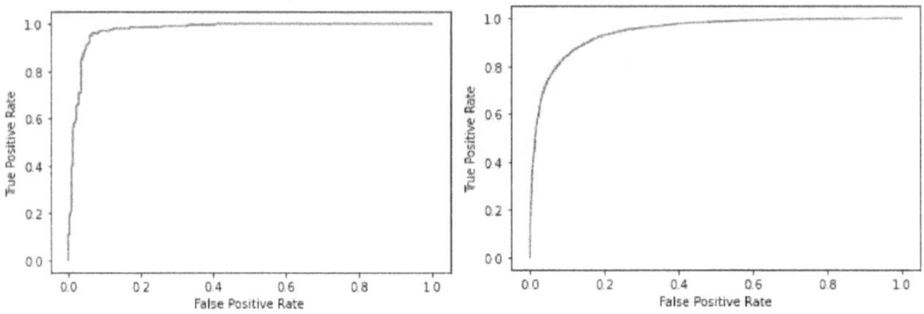

Figure 3.13 ROC Plot prior and following data enhancement

3.4.5 Comparison of suggested methods' outcomes with those of current methods

We evaluated our proposed methods' accuracy against other earlier classification and diagnosis techniques for cucumber leaf disease. The common practice of diagnosing and detecting cucumber plant illnesses using images of the leaves of plants serves as the basis for comparing our proposed model with current techniques. All of the techniques compared here used images of cucumber plant leaf data to detect leaf disease. Deep CNN architectures have been used for disease identification in most of the methods considered in this comparison. The results of our methods were compared using a self-organized map, GLCM model with K-means, SVM classifier with CNN-based features the extraction procedure, modified CNN model, and suggested deep convolution neural network. Images of fundus, citrus, rice, and common plant leaves are all incorporated in this study of comparison. Our findings demonstrated that our suggested approaches outperformed other approaches currently in use. The accuracy of our methods is compared with that of previous methods in Figure 3.14.Unlike existing approaches, the proposed methods can analyses huge datasets efficiently and don't need separate feature extraction modules. The primary issue is that managing these massive datasets would require high performance of GPUs. Since feature extraction in many current methods necessitates manual involvement, they challenge with acquiring the most crucial feature. This problem is resolved by our approach, which automatically extracts features. Some of the existing methodologies discussed in the literature reviews [12],[13],[15] and 139] use automatic feature extraction; nevertheless, our proposed methodology performs better than previous methods because of its efficient deep CNN framework and augmentation technique. Our approach uses the transfer learning method to help identify cucumber plant leaves using their environment.

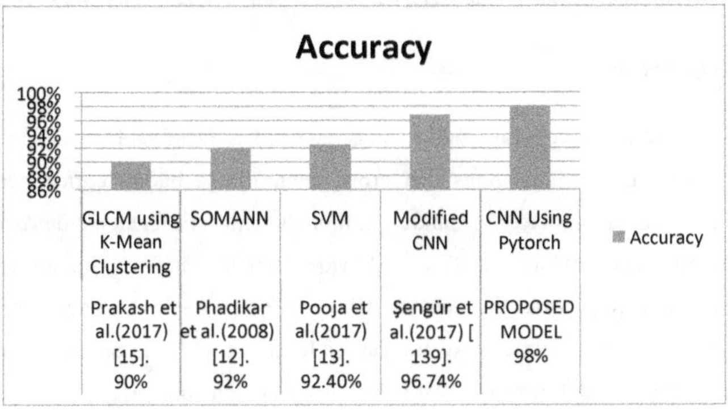

Figure 3.14 Comparison of the accuracy of several models

3.5 Concluding remarks

Plant illness have been recognize and classified utilizing a range of ML method, like SVM, CNN and self-organizing maps, with 90%, 92%, and 95% accuracy rates, respectively. For the objective of enhancing the ResNet50 the model's effectiveness for the specific purpose of detecting cucumber diseases, this work utilizes a Deep-CNN-based illness recognition model. Utilizing a various type of datasets, the model makes use of augmentation of data methods.

By altering the weights of the architecture, over fitting issues are resolved by transfer learning and enhance its performance. Proposed model outperforms current methods with precision rate of 98%. This model's technical specs include an Intel i7 processor 250 GB SSD and 16 GB of RAM.

Depending on the context and dataset, a 98% accuracy rate may be appropriate for some jobs but insufficient for others. Only the final layer is altered after training in the suggested model, which is based on the architecture of ResNet50 and has 50 layers. Analyzing performance of the model on an alternative test set is also very important. The Gabor filter can be employed to the recognition of illnesses in a various type of plants, including coffee, maize, and pumpkin, for the purpose of extract deeper image information.

CHAPTER 4

A HYBRID DEEP CONVOLUTIONAL NEURAL NETWORK (DCNN) FOR COFFEE LEAF ILLNESS CLASSIFICATION

4.1 Introduction

Coffee is a significant agricultural product and is regarded as the second largest industry in the world, behind crude oil. Plantations that grow about fifteen billion coffee trees make a substantial contribution to society. Around 25 million farmers in different nations make a living from coffee production, which satisfies worldwide demand. The two primary species that dominate the commercial coffee business are Arabica (Coffea arabica L.) and Robusta (Coffea canephora) coffee. Robusta coffee may grow at sea level and is also frequently grown in these areas, although Arabica coffee grows best in lush tropical highlands [97].

Brazil is the world's largest coffee grower, contributing 40% of the world's coffee production, with 97.55% of the varieties. Arabica coffee is a profitable substitute for opium manufacturing, having grown in Thailand's mountains since 1849. Because opium is made from the desiccated out latex of plant known as Papaver somniferum, Arabica coffee has shown to be an environmentally friendly substitute to opium production in this area [98].

The most controversial topic in Ethiopia's coffee industry is the switch from growing coffee to using khat (Catha edulis), a stimulant plant that is produced instead of coffee because of its health benefits [99].

The majority of crop is harvested by small, obscure Coffee-growing households, but famines can harm and weaken the plants, resulting in decreased production and a decline in the coffee's flavor and quality [100].

In Marcos et al. (2019), Rust on coffee leaves is a dangerous illness that affects many coffee-growing locations and is identified by orange-yellow, powdery spots. The authors suggested a CNN-based approach for separating coffee leaf rust. To identify the symptoms of rust infection, they trained and developed a Convolutional Neural Network (CNN). An expert-provided collection of 159 images was segmented using CNN. As seen through the large Dice coefficient obtained, the findings demonstrated that the technique could identify the diseased leaf patches coarsely and that employing a straightforward morphological erosion strategy greatly increased detection accuracy [101].

It's difficult for small growers to keep up a consistent flow of high-quality available coffee. Coffee beans of Arabica, which are more popular in foreign markets and have a softer flavor than Canephora (Robusta) coffees, are grown in Colombia. Smaller to medium-sized families that specialize in coffee farming harvest the majority of the crop. On the other hand, plant number and quality may decrease as a result of pest infestations [102].

In many nations, Coffee is a variety of significant economic significance. The goal of the natural coffee crop is to completely avoid using synthetic pesticides and fertilizers, setting it apart from conventional production methods. The control of diseases, particularly coffee rust, that is thought to be the primary ailment of this crop, is one of the most significant drawbacks of the organic system. Coffee rust can result in a 50% decrease in output, which has a big impact on coffee growers' bottom line. Reviewing incorporated rust control of organic coffee crops across producing nations is the goal of this effort [103].

Over the years, both quantity and quality indicators have suffered due to the growing severity of improper agricultural practices. Among the pests that seriously harm coffee plants and eventually affect crop productivity are Coffee Leaf Rust (CLR), Citrus mealy bug with coffee leaf miner, coffee borer beetle (Hypot henemus hampei), Red spiders, coffee stem mites, and roots borer [104],[105].

Rust control may have been aided by the high genetic variety and robust horizontal resistance found in the populations of coffee. Elevation affects the impact of CLR with the disease acting more aggressively at lower elevations and warmer temperatures. The most damaging illness to Coffea arabica plants is still CLR [106], [107].

Coffee leaf rust (CLR) emerged for the first time in 1934 in Ethiopia, despite the fact that it has appeared in other nations for long stretches of time without causing epidemics to spread or destroying particular C. arabica cultivars. Rust and coffee have always gone hand in hand. In 1922, Coffee Berry Disease (CBD) first came to light in Kenya, close to Mount Elgon, west of the Rift Valley. According to some accounts, CBD may harm as much as 75% of crops, which would put a stop to coffee farming west along the valley of the rift and establish the cultivation of tea as the area's main agricultural sector. The disease was unable to spread to the province's highlands, which are Central Africa's main areas for growing coffee, due to the dry environment within the Rift Valley. In 1951, Rayner became the first to record CBD's existence east of the Rift [108], [109].

Brazil has a major advantage over other nations because it is acknowledged by the International Organization for Coffee as the world's top manufacturer of coffee. However, rust, brown spot, and leaf miners are only a few of the biotic pressures that coffee crops must deal with. Defoliation and decreased photosynthesis are the end results of these stresses, which also have an adverse effect on crop output .The tremendous progress made in machine learning's real-world applications has caused the formation of a new class of artificial intelligence models known as deep learning. That is CNN which demonstrated remarkable performance in image recognition tests. As with traditional approaches, CNNs automatically pick up key characteristics using the training dataset, negating the requirement for manually created features based on past knowledge. Furthermore, by including the segmentation stage within their convolution filters, CNNs streamline the procedure. [110].

Instead of categorizing the symptoms and indicators connected to coffee leaves, a threshold method was created to assess them for the purpose of arrange the data. The symptoms were divided into two categories: rust and leaf miner. The elements of these categories were created by hand. Data from the subdivision of lesions demonstrated that signs may be categorized and given a severity rating. Although the outcomes were acceptable, the segmentation method did not take lighting and reflection differences into consideration. The project's main accomplishments are: broadening the collection of images to include more pictures of both healthy and sick coffee leaves; developing a system with multiple tasks to categorize and rate the physiological strain with coffee leaves; and comparing different deep learning algorithms to determine how well they perform when analyzing photos of coffee leaves [111].

A serious phytosanitary hazard to coffee plants is CLR that is brought through the fungal infection Hemileia vastatrix. It is common for the condition to worsen before significant interventions are carried out. Coffee plants that are severely weakened by poor disease control have fewer leaves on their trees and a sharp drop in output and quality. To extract information such as statistical metrics and local binary pattern (LBP) for the purpose of recognizing the coffee plant leaves having lesions, a texture-based pattern recognition system is presented.

Additionally, this algorithm evaluates its detection accuracy against other CNN techniques [112].

4.1.1 Motivation

Black rot, Brown eye spot and Coffee leaf rust are the most typical signs of coffee leaf diseases. Small pale yellow dots on the outermost layer of the leaves are the first signs with coffee leaf rust. With the progression of the disease, these spots get bigger and may be seen on the underneath of the leaves, which vary in hue from orange-yellow to red-orange powdery depending on the region. These leaf diseases may reproduce quickly and cause large financial losses. Thus, early identification of plant diseases is critical. A comprehensive analysis of the traits of the leaf is necessary to distinguish between healthy and unhealthy coffee leaves.

4.1.2 Research Objectives

This research offers a new classification algorithm that uses images of coffee leaves to accurately identify a various type of illnesses, Includes gray leaf spots, leaf blight, and common rust. Convolution neural networks (CNNs), specifically DenseNet121 along with InceptionV3, which were selected due to their balanced parameter sizes, are utilized by the model. Proposed architecture uses combining features to integrate the prediction powers of CNNs, improving classification accuracy and producing a more thorough and precise classification scheme. This chapter's main objective is to detect brown spot disease in rice crops immediately in an effort to avoid losses. The subsequent tasks may have been used to break down the goal:

a) Integrating features from DenseNet121 and InceptionV3 CNNs using feature fusion inside an end-to-end learning framework.
b) Analyzing the suggested model's classification accuracy and contrasting it other models derived from the same dataset, like EfficientNetB0, DenseNet121 and InceptionV3.
c) Improving the proposed model's capacity to recognize and categorize coffee plant illnesses while keeping parameter sizes under control.

4.1.3 Chapter's Structure

Remaining of the chapter comprise of the following sections:
Section 2: In this section some related works are discussed.

Section 3: In this section discusses materials and methods used in proposed "Classifying diseases with Integrated Deep Convolution Neural Networks is what coffee leaves out".

Section 4: This section discusses implementation and results of suggested model.

Section 5: This Section provide summery of suggested work.

4.2 Related Work

This section covers few well-reviewed, efficient methods for estimating the severity of an infection.

In Singh & Kumar (2023)., Since powdery mildewing, downy mildewing, and Alternaria leaf Spots are among the illnesses that can impact cucumber leaves and hinder photosynthesis, it's imperative to identify infections early on to save the plant. By applying data improvement methods on a various type of datasets, Suggested model produces outcomes for cucumber disease diagnosis that are incredibly accurate. A major factor in enhancing the qualities of cucumber leaves is data augmentation. The PyTorch package, which provides a variety pertaining to deep learning methods, was used because changing traditional CNNs required a lot of processing and a huge number of parameters. For the purpose of minimize over fitting and enhance performance, the model also uses transfer learning to modify its weights. The suggested model outperforms current techniques, with a 98% accuracy rate [113].

In Agarwal et al. (2019), the authors highlight the importance of detecting diseases in corn crops to ensure healthy crop production and prevent major yield losses. They propose CNN based method for the automated, efficient, and accurate identification of corn crop illnesses through image analysis. This approach significantly outperforms manual methods by leveraging deep learning methods to handle and interpret image data. The use of CNNs in an important development in agricultural technology is disease detection, which provides a precise, efficient, and scalable solution for monitoring plant health. CNN model created in the work includes three convolutional layers, followed by max pooling layers and fully connected layers. This technology supports early disease detection, reduces reliance on chemical treatments, and promotes improved crop management and sustainable agriculture. The authors designed a classified four varieties of maize leaves using CNN optimization, including three diseased variations: common Leaf blight, corn rust, and leaf spot. The model achieved 94% accuracy after processing data for 1,000 epochs [144].

In Eunice et al.(2022),The authors used CNN-based models that have already been taught to detect plant illnesses accurately. The study concentrated on optimizing the hyper parameters pertaining to widely-used previously trained models, consisting of V4 Inception, VGG-16, and ResNet-50 and Dense Network-121. A total out of 54,305 sample images representing different types of plant diseases in 38 classes were taken into consideration. Advance learning-based method for using image analysis to identify leaf diseases in crops is described. This project's objective is to enhance agricultural operations by precisely recognizing and categorizing different diseases of leaves from photos using cutting-edge deep learning algorithms. A comparison of the results was conducted using comparable cutting-edge research as well. The tests demonstrated that DenseNet-121 had the greatest 99.81 percent categorization accuracy. Extensive studies on a collection of crop leaf images were used to show the usefulness of the model, demonstrating its potential to greatly advance precision agriculture and enhance crop yield by managing diseases [145].

Zhao et al. (2020) suggested an effective method for developing CNN algorithms to extract visual features for identifying crop diseases. However, when processing photos from real-world fields, which often contain noise, these approaches frequently face challenges related to low resilience and accuracy. To deal with this, IoT has become increasingly relevant, providing additional contextual knowledge to improve disease detection systems in practical agricultural environments. The study introduces a novel DL system known as Multi-Context Fusion Network (MCFN), intended to detect agricultural diseases in real-world settings. By utilizing over 50,000 agricultural examples of crop diseases, MCFN extracts robust visual features using a standard CNN backbone. The method shows great potential to enhance precision agriculture and advance automated disease recognition. Using VGG19 pre-trained network, the authors extracted deep characteristics from pictures of potatoes, maize, and tomatoes from the Plant Village dataset. They focused on layers 6 and 7 of the VGG19 model and fused these features using a partial least-squares (PLS) approach. The MCFN approach achieved an impressive 97.5% accuracy in crop disease recognition, outperforming existing methods [152].

In Amin.H et al.(2022), presented a from deep from end to end neural network model intended for maize categorization of leaf diseases.This program automatically detects and categorizes illnesses affecting maize leaves using cutting-edge deep learning techniques. Through feature integration across many convolution neural networks (CNNs), the strategy improves classification performance substantially. The suggested method, which incorporates characteristics from several CNN designs, produced an astounding 98.56% classification accuracy, signifying a significant increase in the precision and effectiveness in corn disease detection [114].

4.3 Methods and Materials

The procedure utilizing image's dataset coffee leaves of healthy and damaged samples—is described in this section. It describes how different features were taken out with feature extraction algorithms from these leaf images. The images are then classified using convolutional neural networks (CNNs) into classes for healthy and diseased individuals. The model is developed and improved through the utilization of transfer learning. The following subsections describe the materials and procedures employed.

4.3.1 Dataset Description

The authors of this work divided 3,076 images of coffee groupings of four healthy leaf groups and three classifications of the plant leaves of damaged foliage: rust, black rot, as well as brown spot of coffee leaf. They did this utilizing Kaggle's Plant Village dataset. Table 4.1 as well as Figure 4.1 provide specifics on the image frequencies and samples, respectively. Tiny pale Spots of yellow on the leaf surfaces' top surface, yellow patches on the leaf and turn form yellow to red along the underside, are an indication of coffee leaf rust. Small chlorotic patches that enlarge to an approximate size of 3/16 through 5/8 inches and turn brown are indicative of brown eye spot disease. Deep brown or black sores on the leaves, which are frequently coated in sclerotia in the petioles and twigs, are indicative of black rot. Using machine learning techniques, the researchers separated the dataset among training and test sets, allocating 20% for testing and 80% for training. A validation subset that was separate from the training set was applied. For adjustment of the the hyper parameters this approach ensures optimal performance and prevents over fitting by evaluating the model on unobserved data. The augmented approaches are displayed in Table 4.2. The images were scaled to the typical 244 $\times$ 244 pixel size for processing.

Type of leaves	Quantity of Images
Rust	408
Black rot	952
Brown eye spot	788
Healthy	928
Total	**3076**

Table 4.1 Total amount of Coffee leaf images utilized in each data' categories

Figure 4.1 Dataset contains illustrations for every category: Brown eye spot, black rot, rust and healthy coffee leaf.

Enhancement	Parameters
Zooming	30%
Rotation	30
Horizontal Flipping of Image	TRUE

Table 4.2 Values for data augmentation to be applied

4.3.2 Classification using CNN

CNN's organizational structure is composed of multiple essential layers:

a. **Input Layer:** It provides a matrix of the original pixel data for processing later.

b. **Convolution Layer:** The layer that follows uses trainable filters to collect characteristics of the image for pattern recognition while performing convolution calculations on the input.
c. **Activation Layer:** An activation function in this layer provides the model with non-linearity, which helps it identify more intricate patterns.
d. **Pooling Layer (Sub sampling Layer):** This part reduces the output's spatial dimensions by utilizing average and max pooling approaches, which lowers the number of parameters and processing requirements.
e. **Fully Connected Layer:** Making connections between each neuron in the existing layer and every neuron in the previous layer enables the model to recognize complex patterns and generate predictions.
f. **Flatten Layer:** This layer creates a one-dimensional vector by flattening the output of the previous level.
g. **Dropout Layer:** By arbitrarily deactivating some neurons during training, this layer improves generalization by preventing over fitting.
h. **Batch Normalization Layer:** To stabilize and quicken the process of training, this section regulates the output from the preceding layer.

CNNs utilize the function known as softmax, which functions as a likelihood distribution function, to accurately classify images. This function determines the probability for every possible class, indicating the chance that the input image fits into a certain group. In Equation 4.1, the softmax method is illustrated. Where $X_i$the data point and N is represents the entire amount of categories.

$$\sigma(x)_i = \frac{e^{X_i}}{\sum_{j=1}^{N} e^{X_j}} for i = 1 \ldots\ldots N and X = (X_1 \ldots\ldots X_N) \qquad (4.1)$$

4.3.3 Procedure for the purpose of extract features

Several layers are utilized to retrieve pertinent data from the photos several convolution and activation layers are usually followed by pooling layers. The categorization module creates a feature map by using the image's pixel values. As their effects are applied to the input, the filters within the convolution layer pick up different image data, between low-level and high-level. Textures, patterns, and edges are some of these characteristics. A tensor typically filters odd-dimensional data by sliding across its input in a window-like manner. The filter values are then multiplied with the relevant window values during the convolution process, and the average of the results is then obtained. The convolution product of the tensor T (input) with F (filter) is shown in Equation 4.2.Here n_w, n_h *and* n_c are dimensions of breadth, height, and channel count, in that order.

$$Conv(T,F)_{m,n} = \sum_{x=1}^{p_h}\sum_{y=1}^{p_w}\sum_{z=1}^{p_c} F_{x,y,z} \times T_{m+x-1,n+y-1,z} \quad (4.2)$$

A non-linear transformation is used on the results of the appropriate convolutional layer via using Rectifier Linear Unit (ReLU) activating function, which is represented by Equation 4.3.

$$F(x) = \max(0, m) \quad (4.3)$$

Equation 4.4 shows how activation layers cause non-linearity in the results obtained through activation function.

$$Conv(T^{[A-1]}, F^{(p)})_{m,n} = \sum_{x=1}^{p_h}\sum_{y=1}^{p_w}\sum_{z=1}^{p_c}(F_{x,y,z} \times T_{m+x-1,n+y-1,z} + b_p^{[A]}) \quad (4.4)$$

Below is the input layer, illustrates $T^{[A-1]}$ along with p_h, p_w *and* p_c layers of activation, they add nonlinearity to the output and are usually defined after convolution layers. Equation 4.5 shows how the output layer is computed, where $F^{(n)}$ shows the filters' dimensions. The layer of input, as seen below compute $T^{[A-1]}$ along with p_h, p_w *and* p_c Activation layers give the output nonlinearity; they are often positioned following convolution layers. The computation of the output layer is shown in Equation 4.5. Where $F^{(n)}$ denotes the dimensions of the filters.

$$T^A = [\ \Psi^{[A]}(\ conv(T^{[A-1]}, F^{(1)}), \ \ldots\ldots \ . \Psi^{[A]}(conv(T^{[A-1]}, F^{n_c^A})] \quad (4.5)$$

4.3.4 The Process of Classification

Assigning the retrieved features to the appropriate categories is the process of classification. All elements are typically connected via completely connected layers, in which each input is connected to each neuron in the activation layer that follows. With several neurons connected to the outcome layer in each layer, this arrangement functions as a classifier. The SoftMax function is shown in Equation 6, which uses its SoftMax activated function to find the highest probabilities and normalizes the output.

$$\sigma(P)_i = \frac{e^{P_i}}{\sum_{i=1}^{k} e^{P_i}} \tag{4.6}$$

4.3.5 The Transfer Learning Approach

An approach of ML called "transfer learning" involves using a model created for foundation one job for another. Usually, one starts with pre-trained models when applying deep learning to problems in image recognition or natural language processing. Neural network models yield significant skill increases, which makes them indispensable for solving issues involving large amounts of computational time. The two most popular transfer learning techniques are model development and pre-training [136].

4.3.6 Crucial Elements of Developing a Model Approach

- Select an abundant data source task where the link among both the input and the output information is well-established.
- Create a Capable Model for This Main Assignment Create a Source Model Next.
- Model Reuse: Depending on the methods employed, the resulting model might get used entirely or in part.
- Input/output Information Model: The model might have to be improved or changed depending on the data that is input and output required for the intended task.

4.3.7 A Suggested Protocol for a Categorization Process

Figure 4.2 shows the suggested task's step-by-step procedure, which consists of three primary phases: preparation of the data, training, and assessment.

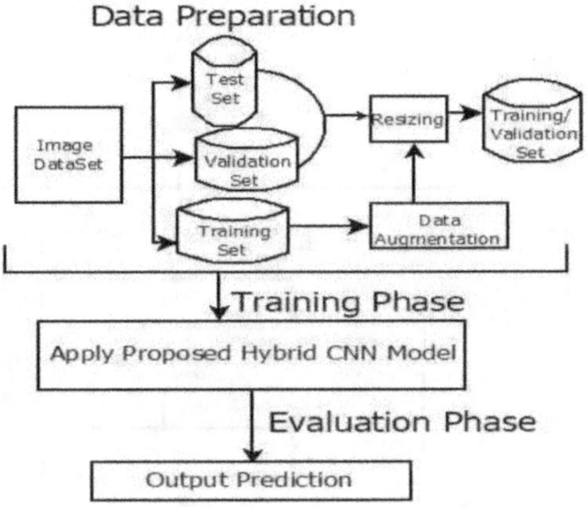

Figure 4.2 Flow diagram of suggested method

4.3.8 Pre-Trained Model Approach

Select the previously trained Source Model. In this investigation, we employed DenseNet121 and InceptionV3, two pre-trained models.

- **Transfer Learning:** Using information from an associated but distinct model, this technique builds a new model on top of an already trained one for the purpose of enhance performance.

- **Fine-tune a model:** An existing model can be made more suitable for a given task by retraining it on a fresh, relevant dataset.

- **Adapted for New Information:** The model is modified to match the new dataset's output classes to the feature extractor's. In this experiment, pre-trained models DenseNet121 and InceptionV3 were both used.

As seen in Figure 4.3, InceptionV3 uses a range of inception modules with different filter widths to capture data at different scales. This model gathers data at many scales by combining these modules with conventional convolutional layers, making it ideal for identifying complex picture patterns [57].

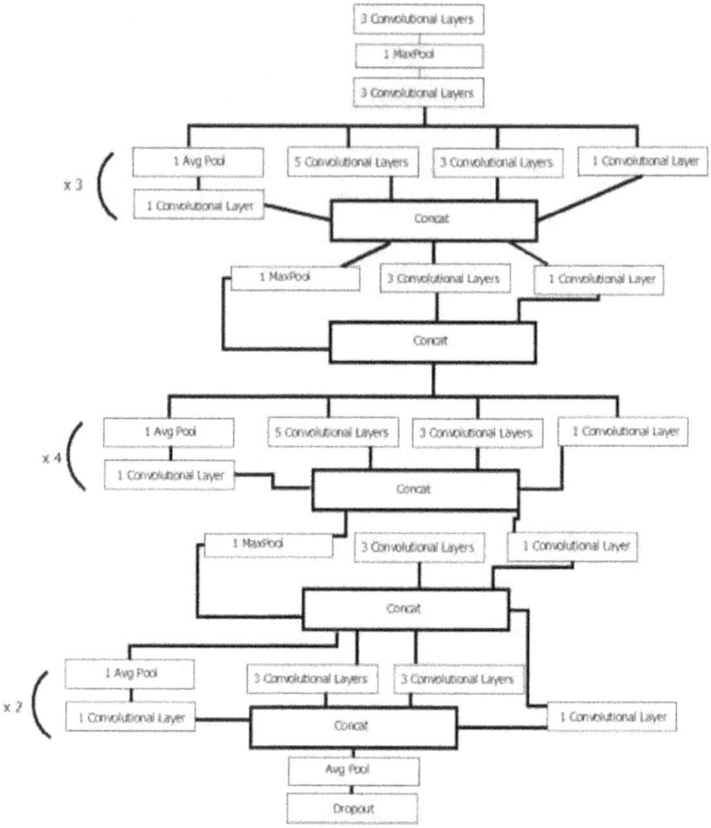

Figure 4.3 InceptionV3 CNN architecture

A starting convolution layer containing three transition layers and four dense blocks make up DenseNet121 architecture. Many layers are densely coupled within each thick block, facilitating effective feature reuse. The input's spatial dimensions are down-sampled and fewer feature maps are utilise in transition layers. As seen in Figure 4.4, following processing through the last dense block, feature maps and final class probabilities are computed using a layer of pooling and softmax activation. Deep neural networks, and DenseNet architectures in particular, frequently include a large block from six dense layers, each of which is composed of a 1x1 layer of convolution and an additional 3x3 convolution layer. This configuration is an essential part of the network's base.

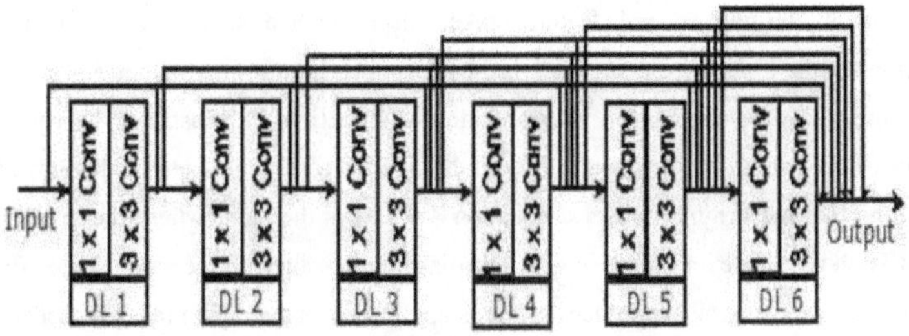

Figure 4.4 Six dense layers on a dense block

The total number of network linkages is displayed in Equation 4.7.

$$xl = H([x_0, x_1, x_2, \ldots \ldots \ldots x_{l-1}]) \qquad (4.7)$$

When the input layers [x0, X1..., xl1-1] are combined to create the output xl, they integrate the feature maps.The DenseNet121 CNN approach, which consists of denser block (DB) and transitions blocks (TB), is a typical DenseNet network, as seen in Figure 4.5 Every dense block has three 3x3 layers of convolution after one 1x1 convolutional layer, and is densely connected. Transition blocks employ a layer of batch normalization, one convolutional layer measuring 1x1. With a 2x2 pooling average layer to establish connections between the dense blocks. The model during this execution consists of four blocks dense layers, each of which, depending on its density, has 6, 12, 16 and 24 respectively.

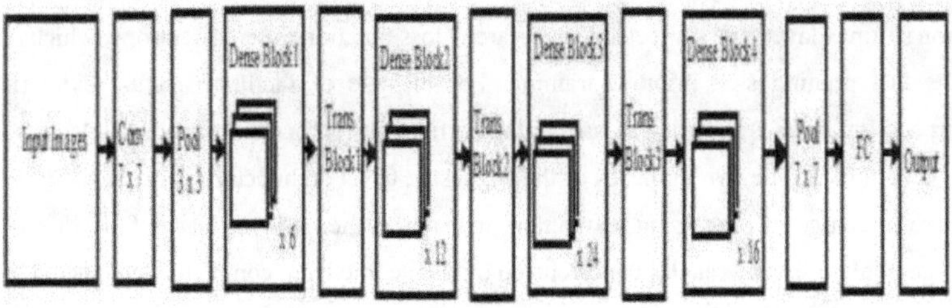

Figure 4.5 DenseNet121 CNN architecture

4.3.9 Feature Fusion

In order to produce a more comprehensive architecture that is useful for a various type of applications, such as recognizing objects, voice recognition and image segmentation. Feature fusion entails merging several features taken from diverse sources or paradigms. The dimensions of the input tensors are analysed by fusion techniques $m_{x,y,d}$ and $n_{x,y,d}$ according to the dimensions are x, y, and d, correspondingly. Equation 4.8 illustrates the way that the elements of each input tensor are merged one by one to create a new tensor that has identical dimensions like the original tensors. Equation 4.9 shows the sum, where the greatest value element is chosen for every input tensor, resulting in a tensor with the same shape. Equation 4.10 represents the average approach, which is applied when averaging takes precedence over maximizing. Equation 4.11 illustrates the concatenation approach, which entails layering the input tensors along a designated axis.

$$Y^{sum}_{x,y,d} = m_{x,y,d} + n_{x,y,d} \tag{4.8}$$

$$Y^{max}_{x,y,d} = \max(m_{x,y,d}\, , n_{x,y,d}) \tag{4.9}$$

$$Y^{avg}_{x,y,d} = avg(m_{x,y,d}\, , n_{x,y,d}) \tag{4.10}$$

$$Y^{concat}_{x,y,2d} = m_{x,y,d}, Y^{concat}_{x,y,2d-1} = q_{x,y,d} \tag{4.11}$$

4.3.10 Training Phase

The suggested model starts the training phase using already trained weights from the CNNs DenseNet121 and InceptionV3. A fully linked layer with 1,024 neurons combines the classification layers, and a median pooling layer comes next. The original branches are replaced by three more completely connected layers with 1,024, 512, and 256 neurons each. The four-neuron softmax layers are subjected to a hierarchy loss function for cross-entropy, which results in the last pruning step prior to training. For the use of facilitate feature extraction, a preprocessing layer is included to handle the particular preprocessing needs of DenseNet121 and InceptionV3. The two branches of the suggested CNN architecture is displayed in Figure 4.6, are in charge of processing, extraction of features, then a layer that is fully linked with average pooling. Each branch's concatenated outputs come from completely connected layers. After passing through a number of linked layers, this aggregated output is finally routed through a softmax classifying layer.

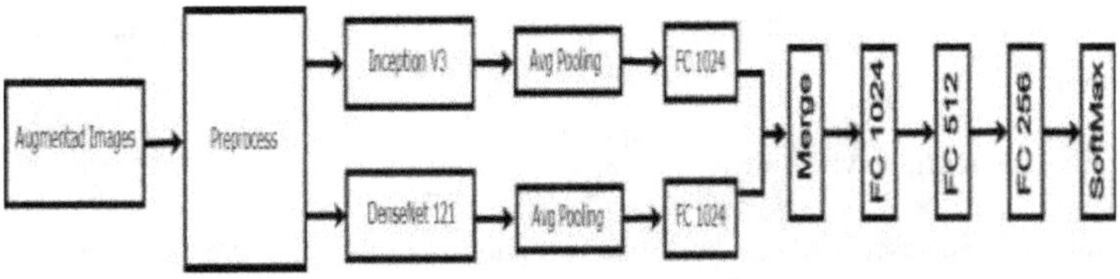

Figure 4.6 Proposed Hybrid CNN architecture

4.3.11 Phase of Evaluation

Assessed the model in the assessment phase to ascertain its efficacy and capacity to address the issue of "over fitting." Here 80% and 20% of the information points within the initial dataset. To perform assessment and training, respectively. Four groups were created from the images collected throughout the evaluation process: Black Rot, Brown Eye Spot, and Rust and Healthy Coffee Leaves. The suggested model made use of the Keras library, which makes the procedure for creating as well as training models easier by providing a large variety of predetermined layers, function activation, loss calculations, optimizers, and utilities. An Intel i7 CPU with a 250GB SSD (Solid-State Drive) and 16GB of memory with random access (RAM) was used to run the architecture. The loss or goal function was cross-entropy, which worked especially well for classification applications. The categorical cross-entropy formula for multi-class issues with K classes is given in Equation 4.12.

$$CE = \sum[y * \log(p)] \tag{4.12}$$

4.4 Results and Conversation

This section outlines the experimental setup and performance analysis of the suggested diagnosis and classification system for coffee plant diseases method. It outlines the experimental environment, including hardware specifications, software details, and the training and validation datasets. Four experiment were setup for this work: first experiment based InceptionV3, second experiment based on DenseNet121, third experiment based on EfficientNetB0 and forth experiment is proposed Hybrid deep convolution neural network based on DenseNet121 and InceptionV3. The section also covers the training and validation processes for all four approaches, a comparison of their results, and a final comparison of the suggested approach with and previous studies. The discussion is organized into five subsections.

4.4.1 Experimental environment

The plant village dataset is where the coffee leaf photos are found. There are three In addition to one group of healthy leaves, this dataset contains three kinds of sick leaves. We have conducted research on coffee dataset, four experiments for the four approaches. In order to validate the architecture, the dataset is separated into 80:20 divisions, with 80%t being utilized for training whereas 20% for testing. All of the experiments are run on a Lenovo laptop features a 1.80 GHz Core i5 CPU. The laptop mentioned above has 250 GB of SSD and 4 GB of DDRAM. This laptop is equipped with Windows 10 OS. In implementation, every experiment is conducted in the Google Colab environment. Tensor Flow and PyTorch libraries are utilize in Python implementation of the suggested Hybrid deep convolution neural network (DCNN) model. The model's performance is assessed using Plant Village repository's coffee leaf dataset. The primary goal of the suggested task was to utilize the Keras library for rapid deep learning model creation.

4.4.2 Observation of training-validation of approach 1

In Experiment 1, original data was fed into the InceptionV3 deep CNN architecture. Here, we have assessed the classification effectiveness of the InceptionV3 model for approach 1.Table 4.1 lists the training-validation samples that were used to experiment with the architecture during its training and validation. At the start in learning, the rate of acquisition was set at 0.01; if the validation loss did not improve after 50 generations, the rate was lowered to 0.1 every five epochs. If 10 successive epochs showed no improvement, the training procedure was ended. Training process and Validation steps are depicted in Figure 4.7. Here, the model's accuracy and loss are plotted against the total amount of epochs throughout the training-validation phase in Figure 4.7. Illustrating the model's performance are using a confusion matrix. Figure 4.8 presents the correct and incorrect classifications of the suggested model for approach 1 using a confusion matrix. General precision of the developed system is indicated in Table. 4.3.

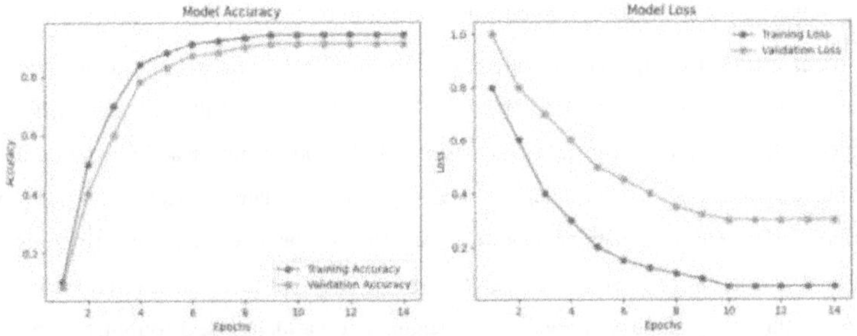

Figure 4.7 Accuracy and Validation Losses for InceptionV3

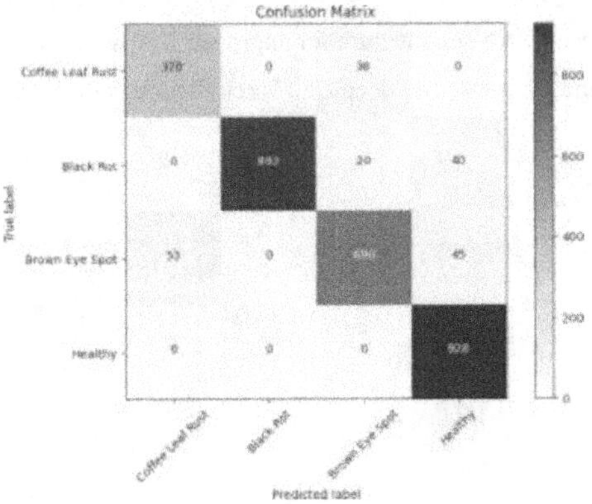

Figure 4.8 Confusion matrix of InceptionV3

Types of leave disease	Precision (%)	Recall (%)	F1-score (%)
Leaf Rust	87	91	89
Rot	100	94	97
Brown Eye Spot	92	88	90
Healthy	92	100	100
		Accuracy	**94%**

Table 4.3 F1-Score, recall, and accuracy of the InceptionV3 models using Coffee leaf Dataset

4.4.3 Observation of training-validation of approach 2

Experiment 2 was accomplished by feeding the DenseNet121 deep CNN architecture with original data. Here, The DenseNet121 model's classification results for approach 2 were examined in this section. The processed dataset with the same training and validation division as displayed in Table 4.1 utilized for training and validate DenseNet121 deep CNN architecture. The same number of epochs, in addition to the same quantity of iterations per epoch as discussed in approach 1, is used to provide learning to the suggested system. Both studies use the same training and validation setup. The validation and training accuracy and loss observed in validation and training is depicted in approach 2 during the validation and training process is in Figure 4.9 with the use of a confusion matrix, right and wrong predictions of the DenseNet121 deep CNN architecture for approach 2 have displayed in Figure. 4.10. The general precision of the DenseNet121 deep CNN architecture is indicated in Table. 4.4.

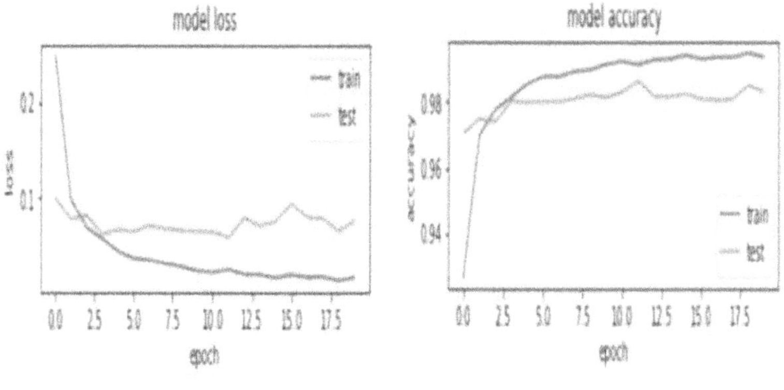

Figure 4.9 Validation Losses and Accuracy for DenseNet121

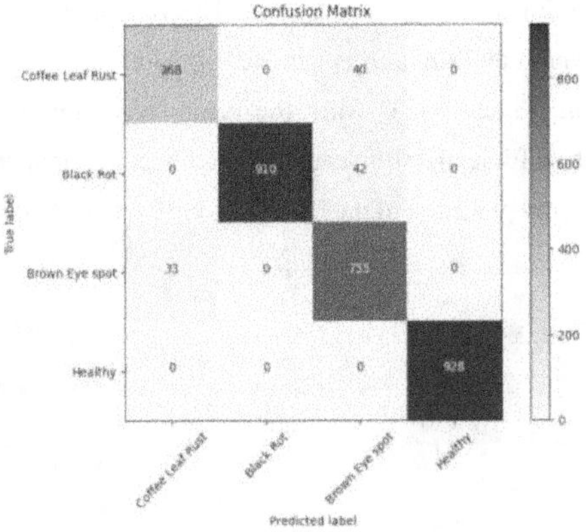

Figure 4.10 Confusion matrix of DenseNet121

Types of leave disease	Precision (%)	Recall (%)	F1-score (%)
Leaf Rust	91	92	92
Rot	96	100	98
Brown Eye Spot	96	90	93
Healthy	100	100	100
		Accuracy	**96.25%**

Table 4.4 F1-Score, recall, and accuracy of the DenseNet121 models using Coffee leaf Dataset

4.4.4 Observation of training-validation of approach 3

Experiment 3 was accomplished by feeding the EfficientNetB0 deep CNN architecture with original data. Here, The EfficientNetB0 model's classification results for approach 3 were examined in this section. The processed dataset with the same training and validation division as displayed in Table 4.1 utilized for training and validate EfficientNetB0 deep CNN architecture. The same number of epochs, in addition to the same quantity of iterations per epoch as discussed in approach 1, is used to provide learning to the suggested system. Both studies use the same training and validation setup. The validation and training accuracy and loss observed in validation and training is depicted in approach 3 during the validation and training process is in Figure 4.11 with the use of a confusion matrix, right and wrong predictions of the EfficientNetB0 deep CNN architecture for approach 3 have displayed in Figure. 4.12. The general precision of the EfficientNetB0 deep CNN architecture is indicated in Table. 4.5.

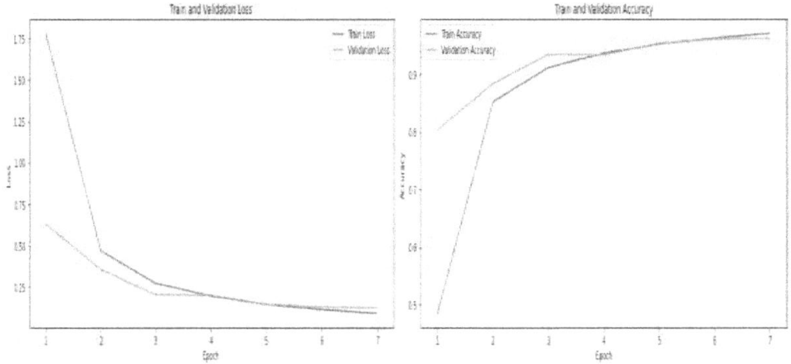

Figure 4.11 Validation Losses and Accuracy for EfficientNetB0

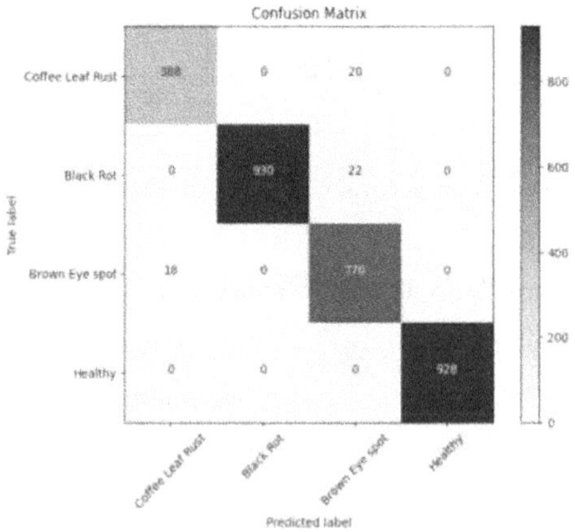

Figure 4.12 Confusion matrix of EfficientNetB0

Types of leave disease	Precision (%)	Recall (%)	F1-score (%)
Leaf Rust	95	96	95
Rot	98	100	99
Brown Eye spot	98	95	96
Healthy	100	100	100
		Accuracy	**98%**

Table 4.5 F1-score, recall, and accuracy of the EfficientNetB0 models using Coffee leaf Dataset

4.4.5 Observation of training-validation of approach 4

Experiment 4 was accomplished by feeding the Proposed Hybrid deep CNN architecture based on DenseNet121 and InceptionV3 with original data. Here, the suggested deep CNN hybrid model's classification results for approach 4 were examined in this section. The processed dataset with the same training and validation division as displayed in Table 4.1 Employed for training and confirm the suggested hybrid deep CNN model. The same number of epochs, in addition to the same quantity of iterations per epoch as discussed in approach 1, is used to provide learning to the suggested system. Both studies use the same training and validation setup. Approach 4 uses a confusion matrix to illustrate the accuracy and loss of the validation and training process. Figure 4.13 shows the accuracy and training process, while Figure 4.14 shows the right and wrong predictions of the suggested hybrid deep CNN architecture for approach 4. The general precision of the suggested hybrid deep CNN model is indicated in Table. 4.6.

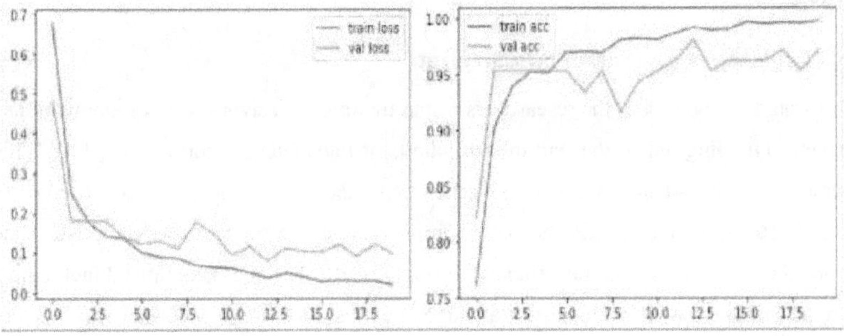

Figure 4.13 Validation Losses and Accuracy for the Proposed Model

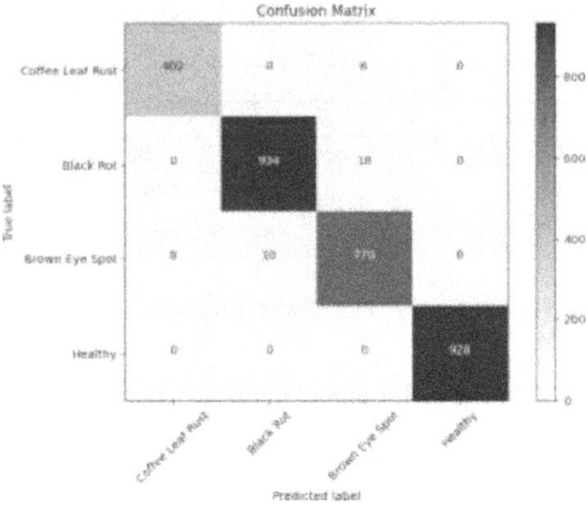

Figure 4.14 Confusion matrix of Suggested Hybrid model

Types of leave disease	Precision (%)	Recall (%)	F1-score (%)
Leaf Rust	98	96	97
Rot	98	100	99
Brown Eye spot	98	97	98
Healthy	100	100	100
		Accuracy	**98.56%**

Table 4.6 F1-score, recall, and accuracy of the proposed model models using Coffee leaf Dataset

4.4.6 Explanation of accuracy measurement

As illustrated in Figure 4.6, the researchers began training their hybrid CNN framework using an enhanced training set. At the start in instruction, the rate of acquisition was set at 0.01; if the validation loss did not improve after 50 generations, the rate was lowered to 0.1 every five epochs. If 10 successive epochs showed no improvement, the training procedure was ended. Additional CNN models, include EfficientNetB0, DenseNet121 and InceptionV3 including the suggested hybrid model were also trained using this methodology.Classifiers frequently employ the evaluation of True (Positives and Negatives) as well as False (Positives and

Negatives) their performance in multi-class classification problems. Using a one-versus-all approach, a confusion matrix may be made for every class, enabling a separate assessment of the performance of every classifier. Effectiveness is quantified utilizing a various type of measures, such as recall, accuracy, precision, and F1 score:

- The overall prediction accuracy of the classifier is evaluated by accuracy.
- Precision measures the proportion of correctly anticipated positive events among all projected positive events.
- Recall is the percentage of accurately anticipated positive occurrences to all positive specimens that actually occur.
- The F1 score integrate recall and precision to give a fair assessment of the classifier's performance.

An efficient assessment and comparison of distinct class classifiers is made possible by the analysis of these measurements for each class, which offers a thorough grasp of the classifier's benefits and drawbacks in categorizing various categories.

i. **Accuracy:** Equation 4.13 calculates the model's proportion of correct forecasts out of all forecasts.

$$Accuracy = \frac{TP + TN}{TP + TN + FP + FN} \quad (4.13)$$

ii. **Precision:** Equation 4.14 states that accuracy is the ratio of accurately predicted favourable outcomes to all favourable forecasts.

$$Precision = \frac{TP}{TP + FP} \quad (4.14)$$

iii. **Recall:** Equation 4.15 is utilized to determine the proportion of right positive predictions to real positive occurrences.

$$Recall = \frac{TP}{TP + FP} \quad (4.15)$$

iv. **F1 score:** In situations where the incorrect classification of positive occurrences is as substantial as that of negative cases, Equation 4.16 illustrates how to apply the F1 score.

$$F1\ score = \frac{(2 * Precision * Recall)}{Precision + Recall} \quad (4.16)$$

4.4.7 ROC curve-based performance measurement

By examining the F1-score, precision, and recall among the trained models InceptionV3, DenseNet121, Efficient Net B0, with the suggested model the models' computational accuracy was assessed. After that, the test data was subjected to the ROC curve to evaluate the predictions produced by the suggested model. The ROC measures a model's ability to make precise forecasts for a given dataset, which indicates the model's overall accuracy of prediction. The rate of false positives (FPR) at different threshold levels is plotted against the recall value to form the diagram shown in Figure 4.15. Equation 4.17 provides an equation for the FPR.

$$FPR = \frac{FP}{FP + TN} \tag{4.17}$$

Utilizing cross-entropy (CE) for a metric, this study closely analysed the discrepancy between actual and expected outputs. Adam's method was applied to improve this difference, lower the cost function, and enhance the model's effectiveness. The CNN was trained by the suggested hybrid model, shown in Figure 6, following the first training period. For a 50 epochs altogether, the starting rate of learning for training was fixed at 0.02; if no improvement was seen after every four generations, the rate of learning was lowered to 0.1. Compared to InceptionV3, DenseNet121, and Efficient Net B0, the findings show that the hybrid architecture that was proposed obtained the greatest Coffee leaf rust's F1 score with the best accuracy. Efficient Net B0, DenseNet121, and InceptionV3 are the hybrid models that are classified into categories like brown eye spots, black rot, leaf rust, and healthy coffee leaves. The recommended model's ROC curve is displayed in Figure 4.17.

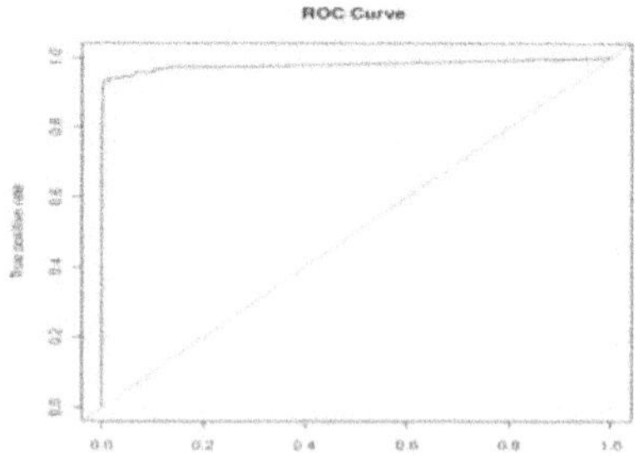

Figure 4.15 ROC curve related to the proposed model

4.4.8 Comparison of accuracy with the related works

The proposed hybrid framework, DenseNet121, EfficientNet B0 and InceptionV3 were all subjected to this process. EfficientNetB0, DenseNet121, and InceptionV3, the hybrid model that was suggested, obtained accuracy in classification of 99%, 98%, 96.25%, and 94%, correspondingly, on the test subset graphs that are presented in Figure 4.9 Together with Efficient Net B0, DenseNet121, and InceptionV3, Table 4.7 shown the accuracy rate of the suggested hybrid model. Tables 4.3, 4.4, 4.5, and 4.6 provide information on the models' recall, precision and F1 scores.

Architecture	Accuracy rate %
InceptionV3	94
EfficientNetB0	98
DenseNet121	96.25
Proposed Hybrid CNN Model	98.56

Table 4.7 Experimental models' accuracy

4.5 Concluding remarks

The findings imply that a mix of intricate feature sets and detailed features acquired using various CNNs is required to increase the accuracy of classification of coffee plant illnesses. In light of the study's conclusions, the model that was given outperformed alternative techniques, obtaining 98.56% classification accuracy. In this work, an accurate model that performed remarkably well with a big dataset was created by combining feature sets with a CNN that had few parameters.

In the future, more diseases will be studied for the purpose of facilitate the early diagnosis of a larger variety of ailments. Furthermore, the model might be even more efficient if further augmentation techniques were applied to improve image detail. For the purpose of achieve better outcomes, future research will also investigate further hybrid approaches and the development of new models by fusing more than two models. This study, which focuses on categorizing frequent diseases that affect coffee plant leaves, has a rather narrow scope. Further methodological advancements are required to address a greater variety of plant leaves types and illnesses.

The technique can be improved for various image types, like fruits and stems, even if the main emphasis is placed on plant leaf images. Additional augmentation techniques could be explored further for the purpose of extract a more complete collection of features. Other insights might be obtained by incorporating a various type of datasets, such as those pertaining to cucumbers, pumpkins, grapes, etc. The use of the suggested model goes beyond producing accurate predictions in contexts pertaining to plants and includes the investigation of biological data relevant to conditions like Parkinson's disease, breast cancer, and other human disorders.

CHAPTER 5

EMPLOYING A CONSTITUTIVE ARTIFICIAL NEURAL NETWORK IMPROVED WITH GABOR FILTERS FOR THE IDENTIFICATION OF PLANT LEAF ILLNESS

5.1 Introduction

In Zhao et al.(2022), To enhance the categorization of plant leaf diseases, the authors create a convolution neural network that integrates a modified Convolution Block Attention Module (CBAM) with residual structures and Inception. They identify three types of agricultural illnesses that harm maize, potatoes, and tomatoes with an astounding overall accuracy of 99.55% by using cutting-edge deep learning techniques. Additionally, they have created and implemented a web-based current time plant illness categorization system in the model that was suggested .RIC-Net model as a classification scheme for plant diseases use to improve disease classification accuracy, this model combines residual structure, embedded attention mechanism, and Inception architecture. The model's efficient extraction and processing of intricate features from images of the leaves of plants improves classification performance. The research indicates that RIC-Net can accurately identify a broad variety of plant illnesses, which makes it a useful tool for managing and diagnosing diseases in agricultural settings [115].

Zhang and Wang (2021) review various models for deep learning, including CNN, highlighting their effectiveness in diagnosing plant diseases from images. The paper explores the datasets commonly used in this field, evaluates model performance, and discusses challenges and future research directions. Since plant diseases negatively impact plant growth, early detection is crucial. While many ML methods have been employed to detect and classify plant illnesses, the emergence pertaining to DL has demonstrate significant potential for improving accuracy. Different deep learning architectures, often paired with techniques for visualization have been developed or adapted to recognize and classify plant disease symptoms. The study assesses these models using various performance indicators and identifies research gaps that, if addressed, could enhance early detection of plant diseases before visible symptoms emerge [116].

There are three important steps in the Trivedi, V. K. et al. (2022) approach. For the purpose of reduce noise from the background in plant images an order of fuzzy (ROF) filtering is applied during the pre-processing stage. In the second step, an innovative min-max hue histogram approach is used to detect illness spots. Using K-means clustering to achieve appropriate segmentation, illness areas must be identified prior to segmentation. Subsequently, in the third stage, the leaf pictures are segmented into uniform sections using K-means clustering and then translated into HSI colour system. The area impacted by the disease is identified as the part with the greatest hue value. Compared to other advanced filters, the ROF filter works better, exhibiting resilience even in the face of high noise levels and preserving clarity up to 95% of the time [117].

One important crop that is necessary for global food security is rice. Rice that is accurately identified and categorized for effective management and increased crop production, plant diseases are crucial. Various rice plant illnesses are automatically detected and classified from leaf photos using sophisticated CNNs. To increase classification accuracy and resilience, conventional CNN techniques are improved through the use of transfer learning and data enhancement. A useful strategy for enhancing the health of rice crops is to use deep learning algorithms. Otsu's global thresholding method is used to binaries images in order to reduce background noise. Three distinct rice diseases are identified by training a fully connected CNN with 4,000 leaf images depicting both healthy and diseased conditions. [118].

For many uses in botany and agriculture, an accurate taxonomy of plant species and illnesses is necessary. Deep convolution neural network (CNN) structure incorporating multistage parallelism for disease identification and leaf species classification. Regarding to collect data at various levels of detail, this method integrates numerous scales of convolution layers, which improves the model's capacity to differentiate between various leaf kinds and disease situations. Through the use of feature extraction at different sizes and parallel processing, the architecture enhances classification performance. In leaf tasks such as classification, this multi-scale parallelism CNN technique delivers great accuracy and robustness, providing a helpful instrument for agriculture study and disease management. Customized filters such as Law's Mask are used for flexible learning since they properly represent surface patterns. Adaptable filters are also used. According to the disease stage, leaf abnormalities might appear in different areas and at different scales. Instead of using a single deep streaming network, a specially designed concurrent multi-scale streaming method with adaptive filters is used to increase efficiency [119].

The CROWDO method is used to address problems including over-fitting, prolonged training times, and considerable energy consumption in an effort to increase efficiency of the already trained AlexNet architecture. Four tomatoes plant diseases—Leaf Molds, Early Blight, Targeted Spot, and Tomatoes Yellow Leaf Curl—as well as the harm two-spotted spider mites cause to leaves are successfully identified by this model. According to experimental findings, with an incredible accuracy of 99.86%, the CROWDO-optimized AlexNet architecture performs better than other pre-trained models like VGG16, GoogleNet, SqueezeNet, and LeNet. Furthermore, the CROWDO-optimized AlexNet has a training time of 12.3654 seconds, which is less than these other pre-trained architectures' training times [120].

To enhance the accuracy of results produced through the Computer-Aided Diagnosis System (CADS), an automated pipeline for the categorisation of plant illness has been devised. A system of expert recommendations has been implemented for the purpose of lessen the need for professional plant pathologists. The method, which focuses on tomato leaf diseases, makes use of datasets from the collection of Plant Village. Transfer learning is utilized for training models of deep neural networks using two datasets: an enhanced dataset including 16,684 photos and the original dataset with 53,476 images. The best successful model was Efficient Net B5, which obtained ideal F1 values of 0.9842 along with 0.9930. YOLOv4 was used to validate the outcomes of Efficient Net B5, and explainable AI techniques were employed in the assessment process [53].

5.1.1 Motivation

The productivity of agriculture and globally food security are seriously threatened by diseases that damage plant leaves. Accurate and early recognition of various plant illnesses is crucial to reducing unnecessary expenditure, economic loss, and environmental impact. For the purpose of recognition of plant leaf illnesses, this study proposes using Gabor filters in combination with a Constitutive Artificial Neural Network (CANN) technique. Feature extraction using Gabor filters improves the precision of recognizing sick plant leaves. To enhance classification results, the suggested method combines a Constitutive Artificial Neural Network and Gabor filters inside an ensemble classification framework. Studies have demonstrated that the incorporation of Gabor filters into a Constitutive Artificial Neural Network enhances the precision of disease identification.

This technique uses Gabor filters to extract textural characteristics from leaf photos, which helps distinguish among both healthy and sick leaves. All things considered, the accuracy of identifying plant leaf diseases is much increased when a Constitutive Artificial Neural Network is combined with Gabor filter feature extraction.

5.1.2 Research Objectives

The major objective of the chapter is to by dividing the disease into three stages—healthy, early-stage, and advanced—the method assists farmers in determining how much insecticide is necessary to treat crop infections. The goal could be divided into the following tasks:

1) **Enhancement of Imagery:** Utilize a Gabor filter on the images to improve and get rid of noise.
2) **Segmenting Images:** Utilize the Adaptive Convex Clustering (ACC) method to segment the improved images.
3) **Feature Deletion:** Continuous Wavelet Transformation and Fast Fourier Transformation should be combined for the purpose of extract significant information from the segmented images.
4) **Grouping:** Utilizing a Constitutive ANN (CANN), classify the input images into several categories. Images of disease-free pumpkin leaves as well as images showing White Blight, Powdery Mildew, Downy Mildew and other diseases are included in the categories.

5.1.3 Chapter's Structure

Remaining of the chapter comprise of the following sections:

Section 2: In this section some related works are discussed.

Section 3: This section discusses materials and methods used in proposed Constitutive Artificial Neural Network-Based Plant Leaf Illness Recognition (PLIR-CANN) technique using the plant village dataset using Gabor Filter.

Section 4: Implementation is covered in this section and results of the suggested model.

Section 5: This Section provide summery of the suggested work.

5.2 Related Work

This section covers a few well-reviewed, practical techniques for estimating the severity of an infection.

In Baser et al. (2023). Authors discuss that, it is essential to diagnose tomato plant illnesses accurately and quickly for the purpose of preserve healthy yields for crops and lower agricultural losses. An improved convolutional neural network (CNN) architecture called "TomConv," created especially with the aim of recognizing illnesses of tomato plant leaves, is presented in this research. By incorporating sophisticated optimizations, TomConv outperforms conventional CNN designs in terms of its capacity to recognize and categorize a wide range of tomato leaf illness. When evaluated against a various type of tomato leaf image datasets, the model outperformed other CNN models regarding precision and efficiency. The suggested method has more capability to be a useful tool that farmers and agricultural specialists, helping to recognize and treat tomato plant diseases early on and eventually improving crop output and health. Using 16,000 images of both healthy and sick tomato leaves, authors tested the TomConv model—which consists of 4 layers of CNN then includes a max pooling layer—and were able to achieve a 98.19% accuracy rate [67].

In Sivalingam et al. (2023), Authors of this study used a deep learning classification technique to forecast leaf diseases. CNN are used for pre-processing and the extraction of features in the process. An RNN-based Long Short-Term Memory (LSTM) technique is then used for classification. When compared to other approaches, the LSTM technique showed best accuracy in recognizing illnesses. They provide a new Recurrent Neural Network (RNN) technique for plant leaf illness prediction. The suggested model efficiently analyses and predicts a range of plant leaf illness by utilizing the sequential information processing capabilities of RNNs and improves forecast accuracy and reliability by refining the RNN architecture and integrating sophisticated pre-processing techniques. The methodology was proven to be more effective in disease prediction than conventional approaches when it was validated on an extensive dataset. Farmers and other agricultural experts can benefit greatly from this novel RNN-based approach, which makes rapid interventions possible and enhances crop management tactics in general. In their research, they trained and classified classifiers utilizing both CNN as well as RNN structures using 20,000 publically available images collected from the Plants Village dataset. Despite the exception of LSTM, the suggested RNN approach outperformed earlier classifiers like random forests, ANN, SVM, and KNN in terms of overall accuracy [121].

In Roy et al. (2023), Authors discuss that, accurately identifying tomato diseases of the leaves is crucial for efficient crop oversight and output optimization in agro-based companies. Regarding to identifying tomato leaf diseases, this research presents "PCA DeepNet," an advance novel method that employs Principal Component Analysis (PCA) and a DNN. The PCA method is employed to simplify the data low complexity of the dataset and maintaining important features. These attributes are then used by the DeepNet model to categorize and recognize different tomato leaf diseases. Extensive datasets were used to test the suggested approach, which demonstrated improved detection efficiency and accuracy over conventional approaches. Agricultural professionals can benefit greatly from PCA DeepNet's powerful solution for better detection of diseases in agricultural settings, which enhances disease management procedures and supports improved crop health and yield. Regarding to diagnose diseases with an accuracy of 99.60%, this study uses a GAN to equate the dataset and construct a quicker region-based convolutional neural network [80].

In Hosny et al. (2023), Authors discuss that accurate agricultural disease management depends on an efficient multiple-class identification of plant leaf illness. This article presents a novel approach to improve disease identification by combining deep convolution neural network (CNN) with data from LBP. To improve illness identification accuracy, a combined technique that combines features obtained from CNN and LBP is suggested. The method offers a thorough categorization framework by utilizing the CNN's deep learning skills and the LBP's capability in texture analysis. The algorithm outperformed conventional methods in reliably classifying different plant leaf illness when tested on a various type of plant leaf datasets. With its strong solution for identifying plant diseases, this fusion technology provides agricultural experts with better disease management and diagnostic skills. The author's merged Local Binary Pattern (LBP) data with high-quality image features extracted using the light-weight convolution deep neural network (CNN) technique. The deep CNN in this work achieved accuracy of 96.6%, 98.5%, as well as 99%, respectively, after being trained and evaluated using datasets containing tomato, grape, along with apple leaves [122].

In Zhang et al. (2023), Authors discuss that, for crop management to be effective, tomato leaf diseases must be accurately identified, especially when working with small sample sets. This research presents IBSA_Net, a network optimized for short datasets that uses transfer learning techniques for disease of tomato leaves identification. IBSA_Net improves the network's capacity to identify different tomato leaf diseases by utilizing pre-trained models to improve learning from a small number of samples. The method shows notable improvements in the accuracy of disease classification even with small sample numbers. IBSA_Net's efficacy was confirmed using a tomato leaf dataset, demonstrating the tool's promise as a dependable instrument for disease identification in agricultural contexts with sparse data availability. To detect tomato leaf diseases, IBSA_Net employs transfer learning and small datasets. The system combines short sample sizes, transfer learning, and Shuffle Attention technique to enhance the depiction of features. The module for Imax is used to enhance The receptive field of the architecture, while Hard Swish activation feature has been added to the ConvBN layer to enhance both steadiness and velocity. Despite the overall poorer accuracy, the technique delivers higher specificity [123].

In Abbas et al. (2021), the authors suggested a unique approach for recognizing tomato plant diseases using transfer learning combined with artificially produced by Conditional GAN. This method discusses the drawbacks of conventional image datasets by employing advanced ML techniques to increase the speed and accuracy of disease recognition. An important development in the diagnosis of plant illnesses is the combination of transfer learning and the creation of synthetic images using C-GAN. By utilizing these technologies, scientists can develop extremely precise and effective models for detecting tomato plant illnesses, enhancing agricultural sustainability and productivity. It is essential to accurately identify tomato plant illnesses in order to maximize productivity and manage crops effectively. By significantly improving identification accuracy and robustness when compared to traditional methods, the strategy shows promise for improving disease control in agriculture. The model, trained on C-GAN-generated tomato leaf images using DenseNet121, classifies images into 10 disease categories, though it shows lower sensitivity [62].

5.3 Methods and Materials

This section outlines the utilisation of a CANN for identifying images of healthy pumpkin leaves and various diseases, including Downy Mildew, White Blight, and Powdery Mildew. The system integrates segmentation, pre-processing, and the extraction of features to ensure accurate disease classification. Additionally, feature extraction with a Gabor filter enhances the precision of identifying diseased plant leaves. These methods and materials are presented in different subsections.

5.3.1 Dataset Description

The 4,000 specimens of pumpkin leaves in the collection are part of a well-known dataset that showcases a range of illnesses that impact pumpkin plants. In addition to photos of healthy pumpkin leaves, it has high-resolution images showing the many stages and symptoms of illnesses like Downy mildew, Powdery mildew, and White blight. Each class of the Table 1.4.3 (chapter 1) displays the dataset. Because the dataset is arranged according to disease kind, supervised learning methods may be used to recognize illnesses. The images undergo pre-processing to improve their quality and remove noise.

5.3.2 Basic steps used in proposed work

The basic steps used in the proposed work are listed below.

1) **Acquisition of Healthy and Infected Leaf Samples:** Pumpkin leaf samples, including those affected by Downy Mildew, Powdery Mildew, White Blight, Moreover healthy leaves are selected from the Plant Village Dataset. These samples are utilized for further processing in this study.
2) **Pre-processing Applied to Collected Samples:** Variational Marginalized Particle Filter (VMPF) is utilise for pre-processing sample images to increase the effectiveness of the input data. VMPF is an essential tool in the pre-treatment process for detection of plant leaf disease, leading to more reliable and accurate disease diagnosis. In this step Gabor filter also apply for more enhancement of features.
3) **Segmenting Images using Adaptive Convex Clustering (ACC):** The division of a digital images into smaller pieces to identifying specific items or information in the photo is known as adaptive convex clustering, and it is used in this stage of image segmentation [22].
4) **Feature extraction:** Applying the Continuous Wavelet Transform as well as Fast Fourier Transform to an image's feature extraction yields an efficient method for processing its frequency and spatial data. We can extract useful features for applications like segmentation and classification from these modifications [124].
5) **Classification using an Essential Artificial Neural Network:** When using a Constitutive Artificial Neural Network for classification, a neural network model is

trained to categorize input images into several pre-defined groups based on extracted attributes [125].

The steps outlined above are further explained in the subsections that follow. Figure 5.1 presents a flow diagram illustrating the proposed approach for diagnosing and classifying healthy and ill images pumpkin leaves.

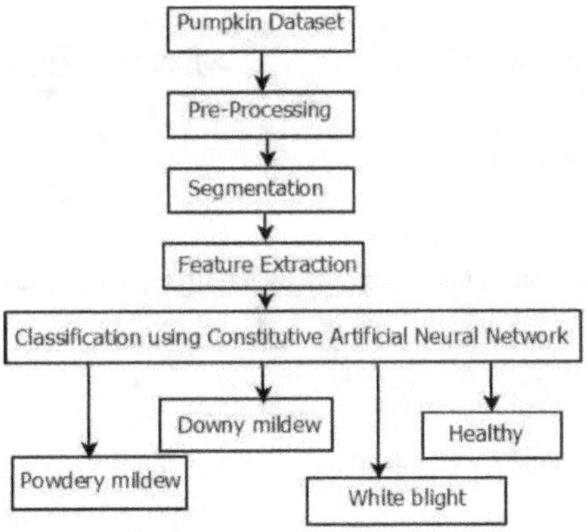

Figure 5.1 Proposed Model for identifying plant leaf illness using Convolutional Artificial Neural Networks

5.3.3 Pre-processing using a VMPF

Step 1: Initialization: Establish the initial values of the particles for i =1,...,n.

$$y^{m,(i)}_{0|-1} \sim x_{y_0}{}^{m}(y^{m}_{0}) \tag{5.1}$$

$$\text{set } \{ y^{m1,(i)}_{0|-1}, X^{(i)}_{0|-1} \} = \{x'^{m1}_{0}, P'_{0}\} \tag{5.2}$$

Step 2: Improvement of the particle filter evaluation: Determine the significance weights for i=1,...,n

$$x''^{(i)}_{t} = x(z_t \,|Y^{m,(i)}_{t}, Z_{t-1}) \tag{5.3}$$

Normalize the evaluation now.

$$x''^{\sim(i)}_t = \frac{x''^{(i)}_t}{\sum_{j=1}^{n} x''^{(j)}_t} \tag{5.4}$$

Step 3: Resupply the resample with n particles.

$$P\,(y^{m,(i)}_t = y^{m,(j)}_{t|t-1}) = x''^{\sim(j)}_t \tag{5.5}$$

Step 4: Gabor filter with update for particle filter time and assessment:

$$G(y_t, z_t, \lambda, \theta, \Psi, \sigma, X) = \exp\left(\frac{-y^2_{1|t} + X^2 z^2_{1|t}}{2\sigma^2}\right) \cos\left(2\pi \frac{y_{1|t}}{\sigma} + \Psi\right) \tag{5.6}$$

$$Y' = y_t \cos\theta + z_t \sin\theta \tag{5.7}$$

$$Z' = -y_t \sin\theta + z_t \cos\theta \tag{5.8}$$

Step 5: Predict the emergence of new particles by modifying the particle filter time.

For i = 1... n.

$$y^{m,(i)}_{t+1|t} \sim x(y^{m}_{t+1|t}, Z_t) \tag{5.9}$$

Once t: =t+1 has been set, go back and repeat step 2. Where

$\lambda(Wavelength)$: The sinusoidal component's wavelength.

$\theta(Orientation)$:The normal direction relative to the Gabor function's parallel stripes.

$\Psi(Phase)$: The phase offset of the sinusoidal function.

$\sigma(Standard\ deviation)$: The Gaussian distribution's standard deviation.

$G(Aspect\ ratio)$: Gaussian envelope modulating a sinusoidal waveform is known as Gabor function.

5.3.4 Segmenting Images Using Adaptive Convex Clustering (ACC)

This step involves segmenting a digital image into smaller parts for the purpose of detect particular items or information inside the image using Adaptive Convex Clustering (ACC). This method assists in categorizing various visual components and extracting pertinent information. Analysing the fundamental makeup of the information, ACC efficiently divides the image being processed into different sections, enabling more precise object or area of interest identification. Moreover, ACC is appropriate for situations where objects differ in size and shape since it can manage complicated and irregular shapes inside the image. Fast and accurate segmentation is made possible by ACC's computational efficiency, especially for large-scale images, which increases processing effectiveness and speed overall. An image segmentation technique for clustering is called adaptive convex clustering. In clustering, comparable points in a picture are grouped together. By reducing the total distance across image points and their respective centroids, standard convex clustering divides data into convex clusters, which is how our method improves upon it. ACC automatically selects a quantity of clusters determined by the complexity of the image, in contrast to conventional approaches that need the amount of clusters to be specified. More accurate segmentation is made possible by this adaptability. ACC divides an image into convex sections according to color and texture when it is utilise for image segmentation. Subsequently, these areas can be used to tasks like tracking, object recognition, and element identification in images.

$$a^{(t+1)} = arg \min \sum_{a^{i}=1}^{m} f(a_{i,z_i}, y_{i,}) + \sum_{j=1\ to\ m} \lambda_j^{(t+1)} J|a_j \tag{5.10}$$

Here $\lambda_j^{(t+1)} \propto \frac{1}{\overline{a_j^t}}$ and a_j^t represent analysed a_j and continue (t+1) whereas λ indicate the penalty weight.

$$.a^{(t+1)} = arg \min \sum_{a^{i}=1}^{m} f(a_{i,z_i}\ y_i + \lambda) \sum_{j=1\ to\ m} \gamma_j^{(t+1)} J|a_j \tag{5.11}$$

Determining the parameters based on the viewed images. The preceding distribution and probability function are proportional to the posterior distribution displayed here as mentioned in equation 5.12.

$$X = p(\beta|y)\alpha p(Z|\beta)p(\beta|\theta) \tag{5.12}$$

In the scenario above, X stands for the data that is observed. The Max_Pos estimate of β may be determined by figuring out. The significance of β that enhance the distribution in the posterior. This could be expressed like this:

$$\mathrm{Max}_{\mathrm{Pos}}(\beta) = \mathrm{arg\_max}p(\beta|y) = \mathrm{arg\_max}p(y|\beta)\mathrm{p}(\beta|\theta) \tag{5.13}$$

More accurate and efficient segmentation results are obtained with this method by utilizing adaptive conventional convex clustering algorithms. Additionally, because of its adaptive nature, this approach may produce dependable Even when there is noise or other disruption, segmentation still occurs and adapt to different types of images. When all is said and done, adaptive classic convex clustering is a practical method for segmenting images with a various type of uses in computer vision.

5.3.5 Feature Extraction Using Continuous Wavelet Transform (CWT)

Retaining only the most pertinent information minimizes data complexity while maintaining the critical traits required for precise illness identification. This is achieved through effective extraction of features. To enhance the efficiency and precision of the ensuing classification algorithms, this step is essential. By examining the image at various scales and frequencies, CWT is utilized to extract features in context of leaf disease in plants detection. This makes it possible to find minute patterns and variances that can point to the existence of illnesses. CWT accentuates aspects that are difficult to notice in the initial spatial domain, like subtle modifications to texture or color that may be indicative of a specific disease, by converting the image data to the wavelet domain. The model's ability to discriminate among healthy and diseased leaves is improved by this multi-scale feature extraction, resulting in a more precise and trustworthy disease diagnosis.

5.3.6 Utilizing a CANN for Classification

Regarding to classify input photos into preset classes using extracted features, a neural network must be trained before utilizing a Constitutive ANN. Model creation, learning, assessment, and data preparation are usually steps in the process. An outline of the procedures for applying CANN to classification is provided below:

Step 1: Feature extraction and data preparation

Apply the Gabor Filter to your dataset to prepare it to undergo extraction of features and pre-processing. Make sure the pre-extracted features have proper labels at this point. Encode labels between single-hot vectors for classification after dividing the data between training and evaluation sets.

Step 2: Create the CANN Architecture

Create the CANN's architecture. CANNs may vary from a basic neural network with feed forward processing to a more complex architecture, depending on how complex the task is.

Build the CANN architecture using the Keras Sequence model. The CANN architecture usually consists of many dense layers using dropout for regularization.

Step 3: Instruction of Models

Utilizing the optimizer developed by Adam and categorical cross-entropy loss, compile the model. Utilizing the training dataset, train the CANN to optimize the network's parameters.

Step 4: Assessing the Model

Utilizing test dataset, assess the trained model to determine how well it classified the images and how accurate it was. This methodical methodology guarantees that each member of CANN is appropriately trained and evaluated, producing categorization results that are dependable and accurate.

5.4 Results and Conversation

In this section, the performance analysis and experimental setup of the proposed pumpkin plant leaf disease diagnosis and classification method. It outlines the experimental environment, including hardware specifications, software details, and the training and validation datasets. Two experiment were setup for this work: first experiment based Plant Leaf Illness Recognition using Constitutive ANN method with Particle after Variational Marginalized Particle Filter (VMFP) and second experiment based on PLDD-CANN method with the Gabor Filter. The section also covers the training and validation processes for both approaches, a comparison of their results, and a final comparison of the suggested approach with and previous studies. The discussion is organized into five subsections.

5.4.1 Experimental environment

Plant Village dataset is the source of the dataset containing pictures of pumpkin plant leaves. There are three In addition to one group of healthy leaves, this dataset contains three kinds of sick leaves. We have conducted research on this dataset, four experiments for the four approaches. In order to validate the model, the dataset is separated into 80:20 divisions, with 80% being employed for training and 20% use for testing. All of the experiments are run on a Lenovo laptop features a 1.80 GHz Core i5 CPU. The laptop mentioned above has 250 GB of SSD and 4 GB of DDRAM. This laptop is equipped with Windows 10 OS. Every experiment is carried out in the Google Colab environment throughout implementation. The proposed constitutive artificial neural network enhanced with Gabor filters (PLDD-CANN) model for detecting pumpkin plant leaf disease is implemented in Python utilizing the Tensor Flow and PyTorch tools. The pumpkin plant dataset of leaves from Plant Village is used to assess the model's performance. The main objective of the proposed study was to rapidly develop a DL model using the Keras framework.

5.4.2 Observation of training-validation of approach 1

Experiment 1 was carried out by feeding the Plant Leaf Illness Recognition using CANN method with Particle after Variational Marginalized Particle Filter (VMFP) deep CNN model with original data. Here, we have implemented Constitutive Artificial Neural Network along with Variational Marginalized Particle Filter (VMFP) model's classification performance for approach 1. Figure 5.2 shows that pumpkin plant leaf disease detection using PLDD-CANN method with Particle after VMFP. In a similar vein, the method also shows excellent accuracy in categorizing the other illnesses related to pumpkins. After using the VMFP particle technique, the retrieved pumpkin images are displayed in Figure 5.2.

Figure 5.2 Outcomes of the proposed PLDD-CANN method with Particle after VMFP on the plant village dataset

5.4.3 Observation of training-validation of approach 2

Experiment 2 was carried out by feeding the Plant Leaf Illness Recognition using CANN method with Particle after along with Gabor filter of deep CNN model with original data. Here, we have implemented Constitutive Artificial Neural Network along with Gabor Filter model's classification performance for approach 2. Figure 5.3 shows that pumpkin plant leaf disease detection using PLDD-CANN method with Gabor filter model.

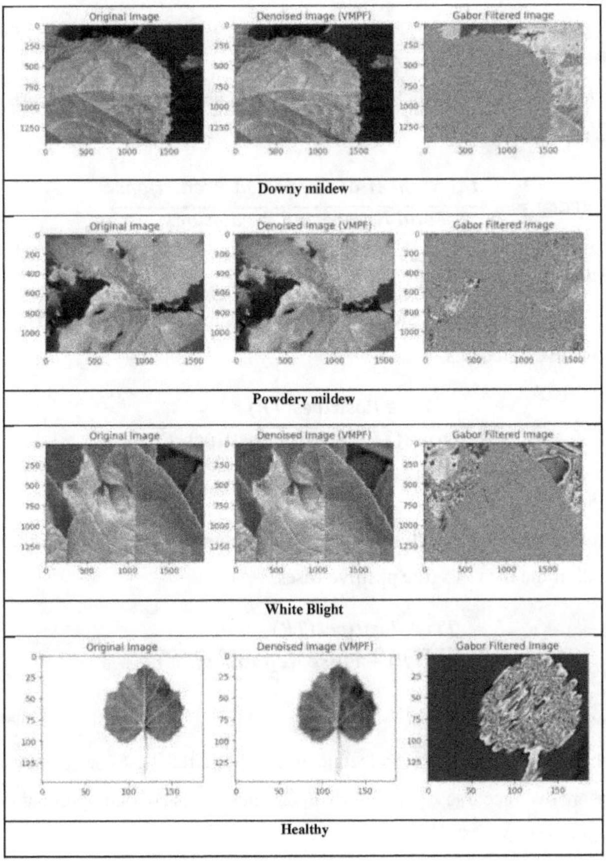

Figure 5.3 Outcomes of the proposed PLDD-CANN method with the Gabor Filter applied to the Plant Village dataset

5.4.4 Explanation of Metrics performance measurement

This section presents the performance evaluation of the recommended model. It includes details about the dataset used for training, the software and hardware requirements for the study, and an analysis of the results.An ANN can be utilize to measure a deep learning strategy for detecting disease of the leaves of plants utilizing a various type of performance criteria. The thorough justifications and applications for every one of these performance indicators are provided below.

1) Accuracy

The percentage of accurately predicted events to all instances is known as accuracy. Equation 5.14 provides an example.

$$Accuracy = \frac{Total\ Number\ of\ Corrected\ Predictions}{Total\ Number\ of\ Predictions} \quad (5.14)$$

2) Precision

Equation 5.15 illustrates that precision is the ratio of accurately anticipated positive events to all expected positive outcomes.

$$Precision = \frac{True\ Positives(TP)}{True\ Positives(TP) + False\ Positives(FP)} \quad (5.15)$$

3) Recall

Equation 5.16 illustrates that recall is defined as the proportion of accurately detected positive cases among all of the dataset's true positive cases.

$$Recall = \frac{True\ Positives(TP)}{True\ Positives(TP) + False\ Negatives(FN)} \quad (5.16)$$

4) F1-Score

The precise harmonic mean for recollection is the weighted F1-Score.It provides a higher effective measure over accuracy, particularly in circumstances containing imbalanced datasets, as illustrated in equation 5.17.

$$F1 - Score\ = 2 \times \frac{Precision \times Recall}{Precision + Recall} \quad (5.17)$$

5.4.5 ROC curve-based performance measurement

A binary classification system's performance is visually depicted by using ROC curve.Area under the curve, known as AUC, serves as an aggregate performance measure across all possible classification thresholds. The proposed CANN model's ROC curve, which is clearly evident at 99.48%, is displayed in Figure 5.4. Encouraging healthy growth requires prompt and precise diagnosis and classification of illnesses affecting pumpkin leaves. Regarding to achieving high performance indicators, the PLDD-CANN technique offers a useful diagnostic tool for plant leaf diseases. This method may attain superior precision, F1-score, The ROC AUC, sensitivity, and specificity while maintaining a low error rate. It does this through the use of focused on preliminary processing in AVMPF, precise segmentation via ACC, disease-specific extraction of features using the Gabor Filter, as well as a highly trained CANN architecture. Instead of just memorizing the training data, the CANN framework and training procedure probably incorporate methods to promote generalization and reduce over fitting, so the model can classify new leaf images with different disease characteristics. Plant leaf diseases can be diagnosed with a success rate of 99.48% when using this method.

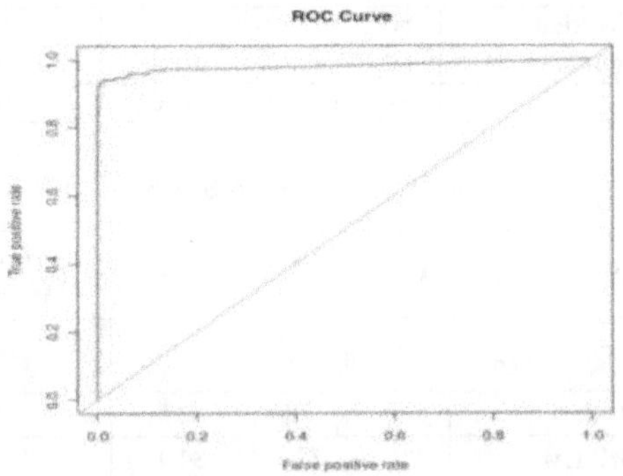

Figure 5.4 Suggested ROC curve of CANN model

5.4.6 Comparison of accuracy with the related works

The accuracy analysis is shown in Table 5.1, with the PLDD-CANN technique achieving an accuracy level 99.89%. It demonstrates higher accuracy in recognizing pumpkin bacterial spots with 98%, 96.75%, as well as 98.56%, respectively, in comparison to the current CNN, RNN, and FRCNN approaches. Table 5.1-5.3 shows the outcomes of the trials carried out with the

Plant Leaf Illness Recognition using CANN method and compares it with other methods currently in use.

Approaches → / Diseases ↓	CNN	RNN	FRCNN	Proposed - CANN Model
	%	%	%	%
Downey Mildew	97	96	98.43	99.88
Powdery Mildew	98	95	97.35	99.89
White Blight	97	96	98.45	99.78
Healthy	100	100	100	100

Table 5.1 Accuracy Score

Approaches → / Diseases ↓	CNN	RNN	FRCNN	Proposed - CANN Model
	%	%	%	%
Downey Mildew	81.3	79	80.5	98.2
Powdery Mildew	80.8	77.2	79.3	99
White Blight	80.4	78.2	78.2	98.2
Healthy	100	100	100	100

Table 5.2 Precision Score

Approaches → / Diseases ↓	CNN	RNN	FRCNN	Proposed - CANN Model
	%	%	%	%
Downey Mildew	80	78	82.5	98
Powdery Mildew	80.5	77.3	84.4	99.25
White Blight	81	78	83	98.2
Healthy	100	100	100	100

Table 5.3 Specificity Score

Encouraging healthy growth requires prompt and precise diagnosis and classification of illnesses affecting pumpkin leaves. For the purpose of achieving high performance indicators, the PLDD-CANN technique offers a useful diagnostic tool for plant leaf diseases. This method may attain superior precision, F1-score, The ROC AUC, sensitivity, and specificity while maintaining a low error rate. It does this through the use of focused on preliminary processing in AVMPF, precise segmentation via ACC, disease-specific extraction of features using the Gabor Filter, as well as a highly trained CANN architecture. Instead of just memorizing the training data, the CANN framework and training procedure probably incorporate methods to promote generalization and reduce over fitting, so the model can classify new leaf images with different disease characteristics. Plant leaf diseases can be diagnosed with a success rate of 99.48% when using this method.

5.4.7 Gabor Filters' Effect on Model Performance

An extra assessment was conducted to compare the outcomes of models training both with and without the addition of Gabor filters in order to reinforce the study. With significant improvements in precision and specificity across all illness classes, the Constitutive Artificial Neural Network (CANN) training without Gabor preprocessing obtained an overall accuracy of 97.62%, while the CANN enhanced using Gabor filters (PLDD-CANN) reached 99.48% accuracy. This performance gain demonstrates that Gabor filtering, which highlights direction-based frequency-specific textural patterns found in sick areas of pumpkin leaves, significantly improves the network's discriminative ability.

Furthermore, the majority of pumpkin leaf infections, including powdery mildew, downy mold, and white blight, show up as specific texture deformations, vein disorganization, as well as oriented lesion streaks rather than extensive color changes, making the use of Gabor filters especially appropriate in the environment of pumpkin leaf disease detection. The Gabor transform is very useful for simulating the minute structural irregularities typical of bacterial and fungal diseases because of its joint spatial–frequency selectivity, which enables it to capture such orientation-specific variations. The PLDD-CANN model achieves increased sensitivity to early illness indications by recording these localized texture responses prior to classification, guaranteeing more dependability in real-world agricultural applications.

The proposed PLDD-CANN algorithm is built in Python using the Pumpkin Plant leaves collection. With a success rate of 99.48%, the system outperforms current techniques like CNN, RNN, supervised learning, and FRCNN for the identification of plant leaf sickness. This study emphasizes the challenges and obstacles encountered while examining the theories and methods employed by various scholars to categorize and identify plant diseases.

The primary objective is to reduce the detrimental impacts of pumpkin leaf diseases on agricultural yield by using image processing techniques. It's also critical that you comprehend the relationship between yield impact and indicators of leaf disease. Classifying and identifying pumpkin leaf diseases is crucial for many agricultural applications, but it may be challenging to comprehend every key concept in the current research. Further studies aim to extend this categorization and recognition of the disease methods to include other plant segments, such as fruits and branches, and to differentiate between various stages of plant diseases.

5.5 Concluding remarks

The Pumpkin Plant Village collection is used to construct the suggested PLDD-CANN algorithm in Python. For the recognition of plant leaf illness, the method outperforms existing methods like CNN, RNN, and FRCNN, with an accuracy of 99.48%. This study highlights the difficulties and barriers faced while reviewing the theories and techniques used by different researchers to classify and diagnose plant illness. The main goal is to use image processing techniques to lessen the negative effects of pumpkin diseases of leaves regarding the productivity of agriculture. Additionally, it's imperative that you understand the connection between leaf disease signs and yield impact. Pumpkin leaf disease classification and identification are important for many horticultural and agricultural uses, however it might be difficult to understand all important idea in the existing work. Subsequent investigations seek to broaden the scope of this classification and identification of the disease methodology to encompass other plant segments, like fruits as well as branches, and to distinguish between several phases of plant illnesses.

CHAPTER 6

A HYBRID METHOD FOR IDENTIFICATION OF CORN LEAF ILLNESS USING RESNET AND CAPSULE NEURAL NETWORKS

6.1 Introduction

Plant diseases significantly impact agricultural crop yields, causing an estimated annual productivity loss of $200 billion worldwide. Advanced methods for machine learning and image processing is very useful for accurate disease identification and targeting precise smart spraying, this method supports sustainable agriculture by minimizing chemical use and encouraging environmentally friendly farming practices [54].

In Bangladesh, maize, often known as corn, is widely grown and used as primary food, animal feed, and a significant driver of the country's rural economy. The viability of numerous associated sectors depends on it because of its extensive use in agricultural, food, and industrial operations. Previously trained DL algorithms along with deep transfer learning shows promising result in the classification of maize illnesses from leaf images. By optimizing existing models, this strategy outperforms conventional methods in precisely identifying several maize illnesses from leaf images [74].

Weeds present a significant challenge to environmental factors and agriculture productivity.The increasing focus on sustainable agriculture has driven the development of advanced technologies for controlling weeds that try to lessen dependency on herbicides. The development of numerous efficient image-based weed detection systems is a result of deep learning's success in a variety of visual tasks [126].

Identifying weeds in plantations of vegetables are more complex than in crops due to the irregular spacing of plants. Research on weed identification in vegetable crops is limited. Traditional methods for weed detection have mainly concentrated on direct identification, which is problematic due to the diversity of weed species [127].

In Burks et al. (2000), the authors explored the utilization of back-propagation of neural networks (BPNNs) in combination with the Colorful Co-occurrence Method (CCM) to classify weed species based on textural data from color images. By using as input variables, CCM texture statistics, the BPNN classifier achieved a combined classification accuracy of 96.7%, with individual species classification accuracies reaching 90.0%. These findings suggest that neural network classification is ideal for situations requiring real-time control, indicating that visual systems are capable of effectively distinguish between plant species and assess weed infestation levels in actual time. The study employed back propagation neural networks to classify weeds using texture statistics from the Co-occurrence Method of Color. Thirty images per class were used to generate input data consisting of 30 texture statistics for a dataset with six classes, including giant foxtail, large crabgrass, and bare soil. Six different BP network models were developed using the texture data, incorporating various hue, HSI (hue, saturation, intensity), and color texture data [142].

Recently, DL techniques using digital images have achieved impressive results in identifying agricultural diseases. A DL methodology was created to recognize in the field of diseased images of corn plants. The non-destructive image capture from field experiments at ICAR-IIMR, India, focused on three major diseases: Leaf Blight, Sheath Blight, and Banded Leaf of Turcicum Maydis. The images, taken with smartphones and digital cameras, featured a various type of backgrounds. To deal with the problem of category imbalance, synthetic images that generated using augmentation method. In this investigation, three distinct structures built using the Inception-v3' network framework were trained employing a baseline training methodology with the collected images of maize diseases [128].

To combat the issue of weeds in agriculture, a method has been developed to identify weeds growing with seedlings using Deep learning (DL) methods. CNN effectively identify weeds that affect plant growth. Various models were created, including architectures with four, six, eight, and thirteen convolutional layers, to enhance accuracy [129].

In Bouguettaya et al. (2021), the authors explore recent advancements in the early identification of crop diseases utilising Unmanned Aerial Vehicles (UAVs) combined with DL methods. They discuss how the integration pertaining to DL algorithms, which can analyse images to detect early disease symptoms, with UAV technology that captures high-resolution aerial imagery offers significant benefits. The review highlights the effectiveness of CNN and other advanced DL models, emphasizing their potential applications in precision crop. The combination of UAVs and deep learning enhances crop monitoring and disease management, enabling timely interventions to minimize crop losses. Since crop diseases can cause substantial yield reductions, accurate early detection and efficient monitoring are essential for maintaining stable yields and food stability. Conventional approaches frequently depend on professional observation, which is useful for small fields but time-consuming and impractical for large-scale crops, leading to missed detections. The study highlights how recent advancements in computer vision and remote sensing, driven by deep learning and UAV technologies, provide promising solutions to these challenges and contribute to improved food production [68].

Crop yields are greatly impacted by plant diseases, so developing an automated method for simple disease identification is crucial. This research intends to help crop growers by allowing them to swiftly detect illnesses to reduce crop loss and prevent their spread, even if they are not experts in plant pathology. To categorize images of maize leaves under one of four types: North leaf blight, common rust, and gray leaf spot, as well as healthy suggested convolution neural network with a lightweight architecture. The training dataset, which consists of 8,506 images of maize leaves in these four categories, is sourced from plant village [130].

In Khan et al. (2020), Authors propose deep CNN method for classifying diseases in fruit leaves. One of the main causes of plant diseases is global agricultural losses, particularly affecting the quality and yield of fruits. To address this, computer vision- based methods have become successful solutions for early recognition and categorisation of plant illnesses. In their study, previously-trained models like AlexNet and VGG are utilized for the purpose of extract features, followed by fine-tuning through transfer learning. The feature vector is generated using an entropy-controlled calculation and then fed into an SVM classifier. A multi-level fusion approach is applied before feature selection, controlled by an entropy-based threshold.

The final feature vector is then classified using a multi-SVM model. The experiments, conducted on the Plant Village dataset, focused on the aforementioned five diseases. Their model achieved a 97.8% accuracy on the Dataset of apple leaves [141].

Dynamic routing between capsules is a key feature that gives Capsule Networks (CapsNet) an advantage over Convolutional Neural Networks (CNNs). This work enhances the depth and performance of CapsNet by introducing a Convolutional Capsule Layer (Conv-Caps Layer), which significantly improves the CapsNet design and boosts its performance. Additionally, a novel pooling technique called Capsule Pool (Caps-Pool) is suggested to lower the quantity of parameters while preserving the full feature representation. In experiments using the larger CIFAR-10 dataset, the Deeper Caps model outperformed all other CapsNet models. Caps-Pool effectively halves the number of parameters between layers without compromising performance and also improves the intuitiveness of the output distribution [131].

Ramesh et al. (2018) achieved remarkable results in developing precise methods for Classification of images based on leaves. The study applies to differentiate between healthy and unhealthy leaves, use Random Forest using the generated datasets. The implementation process consists of four steps: feature extraction, dataset creation, classifier training, and classification. Random Forest is trained on datasets comprising both ill and healthy leaves to categorize the images. In order to extract features, Histogram of oriented gradients (HOG) method is used. Additionally, a hybrid approach combining CapsNet and ResNet is proposed to enhance neural networks' ability to extract and utilize features for crop disease detection. This hybrid DL model, which merges the extraction of features power of ResNets with the spatial awareness of CapsNets, is expected to significantly benefit precision agriculture and sustainable crop management. As technology and research advance, these models are anticipated to be crucial in resolving agricultural issues and guaranteeing the security of food worldwide [140].

Oval and circular lesions on rice leaves are the frequent ailment known as brown spot illness, which is caused by a fungus. It can cause significant crop loss if left untreated. While curing plant diseases, overuse of pesticides raises expenses and damages the environment. Early disease identification reduces crop loss and the need for pesticides. There are two stages to the early diagnosis of brown spot disease method that uses image processing methods to estimate the severity of infection. Based on the determined infection severity, the brown in its early and mature stages spots in the leaf image collection are separated into two groups in the first phase. Fully linked CNN model is created for the purpose of automated extraction of properties and categorization in the second phase [132].

6.1.1 Motivation

Maximization of crop protection and production depend on corn leaf disease detection promotes sustainable agricultural practices, protects farmers' livelihoods, and improves global food security. Improved crop quality, early disease identification, and responsibility for the environment in agriculture are all made possible by developments in disease detection technology. Hybrid models for deep learning are essential for achieving higher accuracy in crop disease detection.

6.1.2 Research Objectives

Main goal of the chapter is to identify the corn leaf diseases using ResNet and Capsule Neural Networks. The goal could be divided into the following tasks:

1. Dual-channel extraction of convolution and capsule features.
2. Two-channel fused features.
3. Image classification

6.1.3 Chapter's Structure

Remaining of the chapter comprise of the following sections:

Section 2: In this section some related works are discussed.

Section 3: This section discusses materials and methods used in proposed "A Hybrid Method for Identification Corn Leaf Illness using ResNet and Capsule Neural Networks".

Section 4: Implementation and results of the suggested model is covered in this section.

Section 5: This Section provide summery of the suggested work.

6.2 Related Work

This section covers a few of well-reviewed, efficient methods for estimating the severity of an infection.

In Malik et al. (2021).,The authors gathered data on five illness of sugarcane plants from fields in different parts of Karnataka in India, using varying lighting and resolution settings. The approach's efficiency in spotting intricate patterns and variances in real-world circumstances was demonstrated by the algorithms trained using this sugarcane dataset, which reached an excellent performance of 93.40% using test set with 76.40% on pictures from several trustworthy internet sources. Additionally, they used Yolo and Faster R-CNN, two object-detection techniques, to precisely locate the affected areas. After being tested with the dataset, both algorithms were ability to get an overall average mean accuracy score of 58.13% [133].

Rice leaf disease detection and prediction have long been major areas of interest in agricultural research. Pattern recognition is currently dominated by deep training and assistance for support vector machine (SVM) technology. When these strategies are combined, the issue is solved efficiently and recognition accuracy is improved. In this work, features related to rice leaf disease are extracted from images utilizing CNN, and the specific disease is then classified and predicted using SVM method. The cross-validation ten times technique is utilized for identifying the SVM model's ideal parameters according to experimental data the deep learning along with SVM combined rice disease identification model has an average accuracy of 96.8% when its kernel factor $k = 50$ and the penalty parameter $p = 1$. Compared to conventional back-propagation neural network models, this accuracy improved. This work presents a fresh strategy for using deep learning to advance crop disease diagnosis research [79].

In Ahmed et al. (2019), the authors focus on identifying diseases in rice leaves to maintain healthy crop yields and ensure food security. They propose an efficient method for automating the recognition and classification of rice leaf illness using machine learning. This approach employs advanced algorithms to analyze images of rice leaf and accurately detect various disease symptoms. These methods provide a precise, effective, and scalable solution for monitoring the health of rice crops by automating the detection and classification process. This strategy enhances crop management practices, encourages sustainable farming by lowering the reliance on chemical treatments, and facilitates early disease diagnosis. Following the required pre-processing, a number of machine learning techniques, such as K-nearest neighbors, the Decision Tree algorithm (J48), Logistic Regression and Naive Bayes were used to train the dataset. Following ten-fold cross-validation, the Decision Tree algorithm's accuracy on the test dataset was over 97%. Three prevalent rice leaf disease such as leaf smut, bacterial leaf blight, and brown spot of rice are identified by this study's machine learning-based approach [153].

In Annabel, L. S. P. et al, (2019), the authors examine and summarize various method for detecting and categorisation viral, fungal, and bacterial plant leaf diseases. Classification algorithms can automatically detect and categorize plant leaf illness based on their morphological behaviours [134].

In Prajapati et al. (2017), using images of sick rice plants, an algorithm for detecting and categorizing rice illnesses is presented. This study focuses on three rice illnesses: bacterial leaf blight, leaf smut, and brown spot. Three segmentation strategies and four backgrounds removal techniques were tested empirically. For the purpose of improving the K-means output, the study suggested removing green pixels from the section of the leaf image that is unhealthy before segmenting the affected area using centroid-feeding-based K-means clustering. Three categories comprised the extracted features: shape, texture, and colour. Using a SVM for multi-class classification, it achieved 73.33% effectiveness on the test dataset and 93.33% performance on the training sample. Additionally, 83.80% and 88.57% accuracy were achieved with five times and ten times cross-validations, respectively [39].

In Singh & Kumar (2024)., Authors suggested a Hybrid model uses the combination and augmentation technique using convolution neural networks (CNN) to merge two deep learning techniques, InceptionV3 as well as DenseNet121 achieves improved performance. This hybrid model is compared in the work to pre-trained CNN models that are currently in use, such as InceptionV3 along with DenseNet121, which have higher processing power and parameter requirements. The hybrid deep CNN model excelled other models, including InceptionV3, EfficientNetB0, with DenseNet121, which obtained accuracy levels of 94%, 98%, with 96.36%, respectively, with an astounding accuracy rate of 99% [135].

6.3 Methods and Materials

This section outlines the use of a Hybrid Method for Detecting Corn Leaf Diseases Using Res-net and Capsule Neural Networks for identifying images of healthy corn leaves and various diseases, including Common rust, Blight and Grey leaf Spot of Corn. The system integrates segmentation, pre-processing, and the extraction of features to ensure accurate disease classification. Additionally, feature extraction with a Convolution block attention module enhances the precision of identifying diseased plant leaves. These methods and materials are presented in different subsections.

6.3.1 Dataset Description

A complete collection of 4,188 images depicting healthy and unhealthy maize leaves can be seen on Kaggle. As shown in Table 1, the dataset includes 1,162 photos of corn leaves in good condition, 1,306 photos of typical rust, 574 photos of grey leaf spot, and 1,146 photos of corn blight along with training and testing sets were split 70:30 at random.

Type of Corn Leafs	Number of Images	Training Images	Testing Images
Corn Blight	1146	802	344
Common rust	1306	914	392
Grey leaf Spot	574	401	173
Healthy Corn Leafs	1162	813	349

Table 6.1 Dataset for corn leaf Healthy and Disease Classifications

Images of healthy and sick leaves of corn are displayed in Figure 6.1.

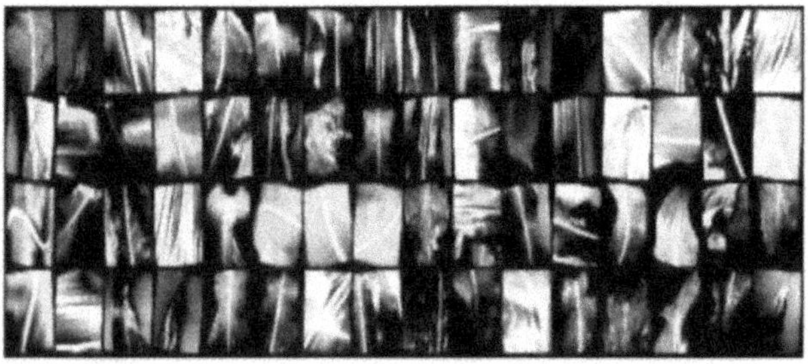

Figure 6.1 Diseased and Healthy Corn Leaf Images

Equation 6.1 indicates the input data that has been applied to the network and the labels of the input matrix in Equation 6.2, where n is the total number of samples, b is the number of classification categories, and a is the input image's dimension. Equation 6.3 displays feature maps, where d and n represent the dimensions and the amount of channel of input image for level l.

$$I = (I_1, I_2, \dots \dots \dots . I_n) \epsilon\ X^{a \times b} \quad (6.1)$$

$$Z = (Z_1, Z_2 \dots \dots Z_n) \epsilon X^{a \times b} \quad (6.2)$$

$$I^l \epsilon\ X^{a_l \times b_l \times c_l} \quad (6.3)$$

The hybrid capsule neural network for corn leaf illnesses recognition, based on ResNet, is depicted in Figure 6.2.

There are three steps in the algorithm:

i. Extracting convolution and capsule features via dual channels.

ii. Fused features with two channels.

iii. Classification of images

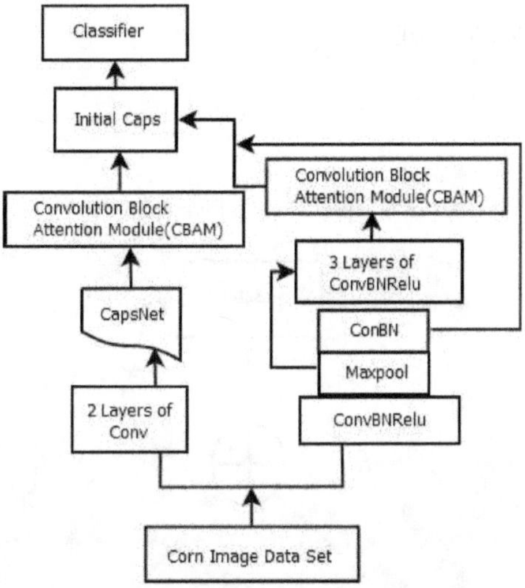

Figure 6.2 Suggested hybrid model of ResNet and Capsule Neural Networks

The capsule network's primary or initial capsules are utilized to extract properties from both input and output vectors, ensuring that extracted characteristics of the primary capsule could correctly route to the appropriate digit capsules through the use of a routing-by-agreement technique.

Equation 6.4 shows the input vector's sum. Vj .where $C_{i,j}$is coupling coefficient, $W_{i,j}$is Weight matrix and $U_i$is prediction vector.

$$Vj = \sum_i C_{i,j} W_{i,j} U_i \tag{6.4}$$

The coupling coefficient $C_{i,j}$can be ascertained. for the starting log prior probability $e^{p_{i,j}}$ Using Softmax Routing, which guarantees the output vector's length representation in Equation 6.5 by utilizing an irregular squashing Equation 6.6 Using the original log prior probability, the final log prior probability $e^{p_{i,j}}$ update in Equation 6.7.

$$C_{i,j} = \frac{e^{p_{i,j}}}{\sum_m e^{p_{i,j}}} \tag{6.5}$$

$$V_j = \frac{||Sr_j||^2}{1 + ||Sr_j||^2} \frac{Sr_j}{||Sr_j||} \tag{6.6}$$

$$p_{i,j} = p_{i,j} + W_{i,j} U_i. \tag{6.7}$$

The dynamic routing mechanism is represented in Figure 6.3.

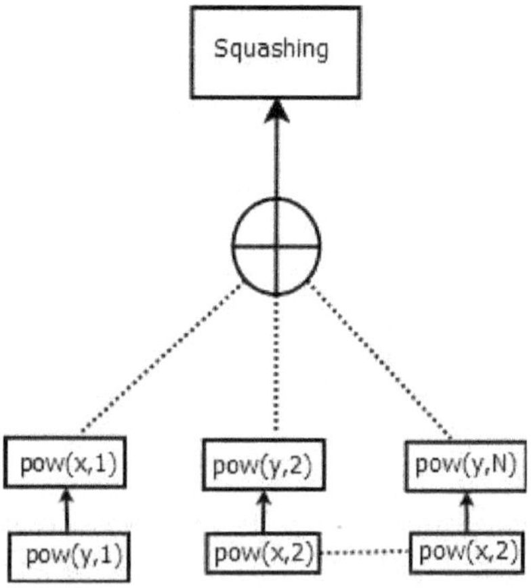

Figure 6.3 Integration of Input vector using dynamic routing

6.3.2 Attention Module of Convolutional Block (AMCB)

AMCB is an enhanced mechanism of attention that works well with current CNN architectures. It improves feature representation by emphasizing both the spatial dimension and the channel aspect. By emphasizing significant parts and inhibiting less relevant ones, this dual attention technique helps the network do tasks including segmentation, identifying objects, and classification of images more efficiently. Figure 6.4 shows the AMCB module's structural layout.

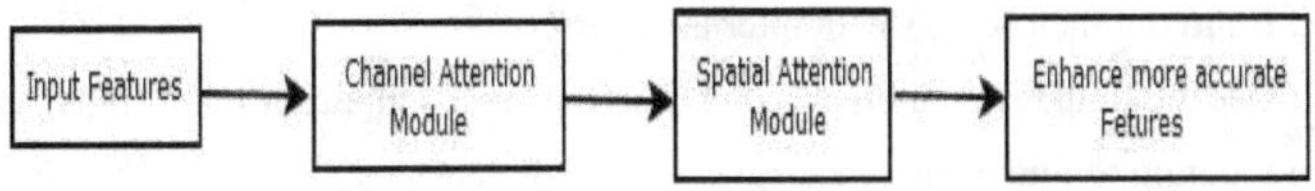

Figure 6.4 Block diagram of Convolution block Attention Module

6.3.3 Feature Fusion

Equation 5 illustrates how the Digit Caps layer uses four neighboring convolution layers with input dimensions. The second layer's output capsule features provide it with additional input as well. It is possible to think of the topmost layer in the capsule network is a collection of several ordinary convolution layers working in parallel. It is formed of the conventional convolution layer and another Primary Caps layer, which sits right above it.

$$I^{l2+1}_{CapsNet} = Relu\left(Conv\left(I^{l2+1}_{CapsNet}\right)\right) \tag{6.7}$$

Semantic information is collected from images using typical convolution neural networks, which do not take the spatial correlations between features into account. On the other hand, although capsule networks take these interactions into consideration, their ability to extract features is limited due to the shallow structure of existing Caps Net structures. For the purpose of improving feature extraction, a feature fusion approach has been created that combines a residual structured neural network combined with capsule network Semantic along with spatial information extraction is strength of the combination capsule. With this method, The fused capsule absorbs the role of the 4D model, producing fused features f_j Equation 6.8 illustrates how the information $I^{l2+1}_{CapsNet}$ obtained from the neural network's I^{l1}_{j} and the previous capsule network are combined using the intersection approach to create these fused features.

$$f_j = g(I^{l1}_j) \cup I^{l2+1}_{CapsNet} \quad (6.8)$$

6.3.4 Algorithm of Proposed Hybrid Model

Step 1: Input images I provide to the network.

Step 2: Use a traditional convolution layer to extract the first low-level features, then map them to principal features.

Step 3: Reshape the principal feature maps to main capsules after applying several parallel convolution layers to create primary capsules.

Step 4: Build remnant blocks with internal layers.

Step 5: Use the final residual block's output as the layer's input for Digit Caps, which uses dynamic routing to join primary capsules with digit capsules.

Step 6: Apply a classifier to the output of the Digit Caps layer.

6.4 Results and Conversation

In this section, the performance analysis and experimental setup of the proposed hybrid method for identification of corn leaf illness using ResNet and Capsule Neural Networks method. It outlines the experimental environment, including hardware specifications, software details, and the training and validation datasets. Experiment were setup for this work: based Corn Plant Leaf Illness Identification using Hybrid method of ResNet and Capsule Neural Networks. The section also covers the training and validation processes for both approaches, a comparison of their results, and a final comparison between the suggested approach and previous studies. The discussion is organized into five subsections.

6.4.1 Experimental environment

Through the Plant Village dataset, the dataset containing images of corn plant leaves was acquired. There are three In addition to one group of healthy leaves, this dataset contains three kinds of sick leaves. To validate the model, the dataset is divided into 70:30 divisions, with 70% of the dataset being used for training and 30% for testing. All of the experiments are run on a Lenovo laptop features a 1.80 GHz Core i5 CPU. The laptop mentioned above has 250 GB of SSD and 4 GB of DDRAM. This laptop is equipped with Windows 10 OS. In implementation, every experiment is carried out in Google Colab environment. Tensor Flow and PyTorch libraries are utilize in Python implementation of the suggested corn plant leaf illness identification using Hybrid method of ResNet and Capsule Neural Networks deep convolution neural network model. The model's performance is assessed using the Plant Village repository's corn plant leaf dataset. The main aim of the proposed work was to rapidly develop a DL model using the Keras framework.

6.4.2 Observation of training-validation of approach

A classification network's capacity to extract features—a critical component for precise classification—determines a great deal of its performance. This method uses a feature fusion technique to merge the features extracted inside the capsule with those obtained using convolution. This makes it possible to concentrate on the image's semantic and spatial elements more successfully. The capacity to distinguish between classes is improved by the fused features' more complete information, which leads to more precise feature extraction for the categorization of maize leaf diseases.Figures 6.5 and 6.6 shows the training and validation accuracy loss of the suggested hybrid model. Confusion matrix is displayed in Figure 6.7, the hybrid model can enhance recognition accuracy and extract more detailed visual information by combining the convolution neural network layer with improved feature extraction.

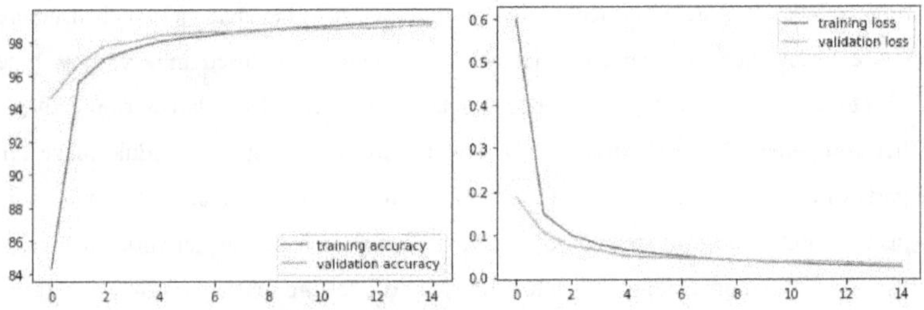

Figure 6.5 Accuracy and Loss of Proposed Hybrid model of ResNet and Capsule Neural Networks

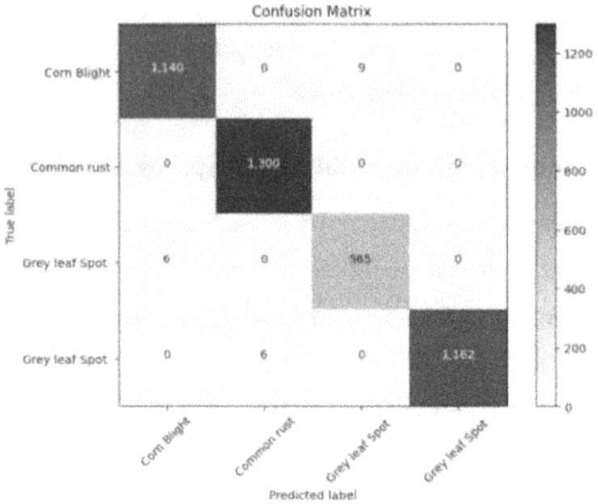

Figure 6.6 Confusion matrix of proposed hybrid model of ResNet and capsule neural networks'

6.4.3 Explanation of Metrics performance measurement

Performance indicators are numerical indicators that are used to evaluate a model, structure, or process's efficacy, accuracy, and efficiency. These metrics are used in a various type of industries to assess a system's performance against predetermined standards or objectives.The classifier component, feature extraction framework, and feature fusion module make up the three parts of the suggested network. The primary module for feature extraction uses parallel dual-channel architecture to extract features for convolution neural networks with capsule features. The four-dimensional capsule channels of feature extraction have a layer of convolution outside the primary layer and four convolution layers inside. The convolution extraction of features channel consists of four blocks of residual, a Normalizing of Batches (BN), a convolution level, and a Function of Linear Rectification. After combining the attributes of each of the channels. Thus, the feature fusion part goes ahead and categorizes these capsules.Recall, accuracy, precision, and F1 score are employed to gauge how successfully the models recognize data. Common Performance Measures for Deep Learning are given below

1) **Accuracy:** The proportion of cases out of all instances that were successfully predicted. As illustrated in Equation 6.9.

$$\textbf{Accuracy} = \frac{True(Positive) + True(Negative)}{True(Positive) + False(Positive) + True(Negative) + False(Negative)} \quad (6.9)$$

2) **Precision:** The fraction of all optimistic forecasts that are actually positive predictions is known as precision that shown in Equation 6.10.

$$Precision = \frac{True(Positive)}{True(Positive) + False(Positive)} \quad (6.10)$$

3) .**Recall:** The percentage of real positives found out of all real positives is known as recall (sensitivity). As illustrated in Equation 6.11.

$$Recall = \frac{True(Positive)}{True(Positive) + False(Negative)} \quad (6.11)$$

4) **F1-Score:** Equation 6.12 shows that Recall and precision are balanced by the harmonic mean of the two variables that is ROC-AUC curve measures the trade-off between true positive and false positive rates.

$$F1\ Score = 2 \times\times \frac{Precision \times Recall}{Precision + Recall} \quad (6.12)$$

Equations 6.9, 6.10, 6.11, and 6.12 show how to assess how well categorization models

6.4.4 Classification performance

Three classifications of corn leaf illness are identified with proposed hybrid model and compared with other existing models such as PaddyLeaf15 CNN (Biradar et al., 2022), CapsNet (Sabour et al., 2017), and RESCapsNet (Zhang, X. et al.,2024).

The table 6.2 below shows the overall performance of these models, with the proposed hybrid model demonstrating superior performance compared to the others. The classification accuracy for three different forms of corn leaf diseases is displayed in Figure 6.8, which contrasts the suggested hybrid model with RESCapsNet.

Approaches	Training Accuracy	Testing Accuracy	Precision	Recall	F1-Score

PaddyLeaf15 CNN (Biradar et al., 2022) [150]	95 %	93 %	94 %	94 %	92 %
CapsNet(Sabour et al., 2017) [60]	88.34 %	87.06 %	87 %	87 %	87 %
RESCapsNet (Zhang, X. et al.,2024)[151]	99.44 %	98.82 %	98.8 %	98.9 %	98.8 %
Proposed Hybrid Model	99.81 %	99.63 %	99.6 %	99.7 %	99.6 %

Table 6.2 Four models' performances are compared

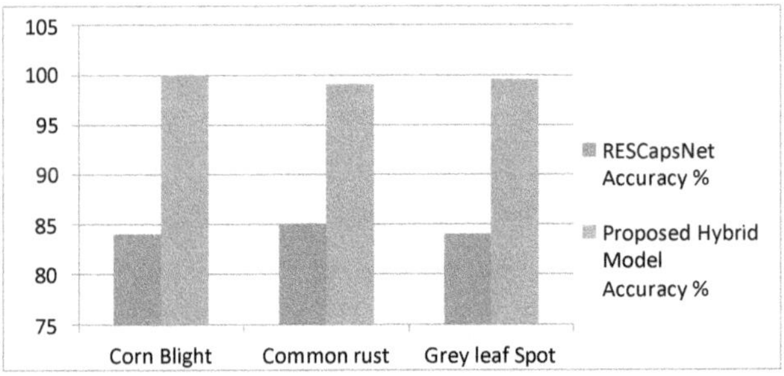

Figure 6.7 Three corn leaf diseases' classification accuracy on RESCapsNet and proposed Hybrid model is demonstrated

6.5 Concluding remarks

The suggested Deep Learning Hybrid model uses two distinct channels for extracting features and presents a clearly defined feature fusion method that combines semantic and spatial data. Three different kinds of maize leaf illnesses were taken by the Kaggle knowledge pool and used to construct a dataset that this model could use for recognizing corn leaf diseases. The study's findings show that, when it came to identifying maize leaf diseases, the suggested hybrid model scored 99.6% on its F1 score and 99.56% accuracy rate. This indicates a 12.54% increase in accuracy over CapsNet, improving the model's suitability for practical uses and increasing the amount of corn produced per acre. To make the suggested hybrid model even more useful for everyday use, more work must be done to decrease its size and increase its identification accuracy.

CHAPTER 7

CONCLUSION & FUTURE WORK

Plant infections have a big influence on the security and security of food. Research on plant diseases, with an emphasis on their impact on agricultural production and crop security, is crucial given the growing world population with increasing demand for food. Several approaches have been suggested for plant illness identification using hyper-heuristic methods. Among these, Deep learning has become the favoured solution due to its impressive results. Deep Convolution Neural Networks (DCNNs) are essential to contemporary machine learning and artificial intelligence because of their capacity to handle complicated visual input in an efficient manner. DCNNs are essential to the advancement of visual identification and interpretation technology, propelling innovation in a wide range of disciplines. Additionally, DCNNs improve plant disease detection systems' efficacy and efficiency, which helps with crop management, yield optimization, and food security.

This chapter summarizes the thesis's primary contributions and suggests further study avenues. The thesis's last thoughts are presented in Section 7.1, while suggestions for furthering studies on the recognition of plant leaf illnesses are given in Section 7.2.

7.1 Conclusion

By identifying current research gaps through a review of the literature, we developed and tested four different architectures for the recognition of plant leaf illnesses. First of all we investigated whether cucumber plant illnesses could be identified and classified using leaf images using a simple fully linked Convolution Neural Network (CNN) architecture. We also looked into whether using a background removal method could improve the model's functionality even more. The first research goal of this thesis is satisfied by this research. In this work we have used 3700 images of four categories such as Powdery mildew, Downy mildew, Alternaria leaf spot and healthy cucumber leaves. After augmentation of these features of these images were improve then dataset divided into 67% and 33% in training and testing respectively then we adjusted the weight in transfer learning phase for improve the performance of model and over fitting problem. Finally, we utilized a deep CNN to enhance the performance of ResNet. In this work we use high configuration hardware such as Intel i7 processor along with 250 GB SSD and 16 GB. We observed that the proposed deep convolution neural network achieved a superior accuracy of 98% compared to support vector machines (SVM) at 90%, self-organizing maps (SOM) at 92%, and convolution neural networks (CNNs) at 95%.

In the second phase of research, we focused on coffee disease, utilizing 3,076 images that included healthy leaves and three types of coffee leaf diseases: Brown Eye Spot, Leaf Rust, and Black Spot. The proposed Hybrid CNN model was developed using the Keras library, which contain several layers, function activation, function of loss, optimizers, and utilities, making the process of building and training models more efficient. This model has an Intel i7 CPU and a 250 GB solid-state drive (SSD) as well as up to 16 GB of random-access memory (RAM) for storing data. In this work, we employed InceptionV3 along with DenseNet121 as pre-trained models, especially in the assessment phase, to gauge their efficacy and capacity to avoid the "over fitting" problem. 20% of the dataset was set aside for testing and the remaining 80% for training. A robust model was created in this study by combining feature sets with a CNN that had only a few parameters. The suggested model performed better than alternative techniques, with 99% classification accuracy.

In the third phase of research, we focused on corn disease, utilizing 4,188 images that included healthy leaves and three types of corn leaf diseases: Corn Blight, Common rust and Grey leaf Spot. The proposed model's strength lies in three key modules: the classifier component, the feature fusion module, and the feature extraction framework. Convolution neural network was employed to extract features from the given image dataset, and subsequently, the feature fusion method categorized these features into spatial and semantic data. The proposed Hybrid CNN model based on ResNet and Capsule Neural Network was developed using the Keras library, which contain several layers, function activation, function of loss, optimizers, and utilities, making the process of building and training models more efficient. This model has an Intel i7 CPU and a 250 GB solid-state drive (SSD) as well as up to 16 GB of random-access memory (RAM) for storing data. In this work, we employed ResNet along with Capsule Neural Network as pre-trained models, especially in the assessment phase, to gauge their efficacy and capacity to avoid the "over fitting" problem. 30% of the dataset was set aside for testing and the remaining 70% for training. A robust model was created in this study by combining feature sets with a CNN that had only a few parameters. The suggested model performed better than alternative techniques, with 99.56% classification accuracy. Proposed model improve 12.54% accuracy than Caps Net.

In the fourth phase of research, we focused on Pumpkin leaf diseases, utilizing a dataset of 4,000 images that included healthy leaves and three types of diseased samples: Downy Mildew, Powdery Mildew, and White Blight. The proposed model's strength lies in three critical modules: the classifier component, the feature fusion module, and the feature extraction framework. During pre-processing, we incorporated the Gabor filter method to extract more refined features, aiming to enhance our classification accuracy. After which the feature fusion method categorized these features into spatial and semantic data. The model's robustness is further enhanced by employing the Variational Marginalized Particle Filter (VMPF) for pre-processing the sample images, improving the input data quality. These pre-processed images are then segmented using Adaptive Convex Clustering. Essential features are extracted using Continuous Wavelet Transform and Fast Fourier Transform. Finally, a Constitutive Artificial Neural Network is used for the classification of healthy and diseased images. This model has an Intel i7 CPU and a 250 GB solid-state drive (SSD) as well as up to 16 GB of random-access memory (RAM) for storing data. In this work, "Detecting Plant Leaf Diseases through a Constitutive Artificial Neural Network Utilizing Gabor Filters," the combination of Gabor Filters with the Constitutive Artificial Neural Network yielded a promising result, achieving a 99.48% classification accuracy, surpassing existing techniques.

7.2 Future Work

1. This work mainly focuses on detecting and classifying plant leaf diseases, with plans to shift emphasis to fruits and flowers in the future.
2. This study focus on concentrating solely on detecting a single disease per plant leaf. In future plan, expanding this work to address multiple diseases on a single leaf.
3. This study focus on two deep convolution neural network architectures. Moving forward, future plan to use more than two deep convolution neural architectures in conjunction with various filtering techniques to achieve more accurate results.
4. Future plan to be to develop an IoT system to automatically collect real-time data.

www.ingramcontent.com/pod-product-compliance
Lightning Source LLC
LaVergne TN
LVHW010730061126
851857LV00014B/1421
* 9 7 8 1 9 6 2 1 1 6 6 0 2 *